Famous Freaks

Famous Freaks

Weird and Shocking Facts About Famous Figures

Deborah Warren

Skyhorse Publishing

All Rights Reserved. No part of this book may be reproduced in any manner without the express written consent of the publisher, except in the case of brief excerpts in critical reviews or articles. All inquiries should be addressed to Skyhorse Publishing, 307 West 36th Street, 11th Floor, New York, NY 10018.

Skyhorse Publishing books may be purchased in bulk at special discounts for sales promotion, corporate gifts, fund-raising, or educational purposes. Special editions can also be created to specifications. For details, contact the Special Sales Department, Skyhorse Publishing, 307 West 36th Street, 11th Floor, New York, NY 10018 or info@ skyhorsepublishing.com.

Skyhorse® and Skyhorse Publishing® are registered trademarks of Skyhorse Publishing, Inc.®, a Delaware corporation.

Visit our website at www.skyhorsepublishing.com.
Please follow our publisher Tony Lyons on Instagram @tonylyonsisuncertain

10 9 8 7 6 5 4 3 2 1

Library of Congress Cataloging-in-Publication Data is available on file.

Print ISBN: 978-1-5107-7867-2
eBook ISBN: 978-1-5107-7930-3

Cover design by David Ter-Avanesyan

Printed in the United States of America

Dedicated to The Order of the Guinness Candle

CONTENTS

XI
INTRODUCTION

1
ROYALTY IN WESTERN HISTORY

15
ANCIENT KINGS

29
TYRANTS AND DICTATORS

43
CRIMINALS AND PSYCHOPATHS

47
QUACKS AND CHEATERS

51
AMERICAN GOVERNMENT FIGURES

55
US PRESIDENTS

73
BRITISH POLITICAL LEADERS

75
MILITARY

79
BARBARIAN RAIDERS (EUROPE AND THE EAST)

85
SCIENTISTS

105
TECHNOLOGY

109
PRIMATOLOGISTS

111
MEDICINE

115
PHILOSOPHERS

121
ATHLETES

125
WRITERS

143
POETS

151
THE SUPER-RICH

155
EXPLORERS

159
FASHION DESIGNERS

163
ARTISTS

169
MUSICIANS

173
CLASSICAL COMPOSERS

177
VARIOUS RELIGIOUS TYPES

185
SELECTED SAINTS

189
ODDS AND ENDS

INTRODUCTION

Thomas Edison proposed to his wife in Morse code.

The *Institut Pasteur* verified some of Renoir's paintings from their traces of cat fur.

The Haitian president, Duvalier, had the air above John F. Kennedy's tomb brought to him in an effort to control JFK's soul.

Coco Chanel worked for the Abwehr, a German military-intelligence service, as Agent F-7124, codename "Westminster"—fashion *and* fascism.

This book is a deluge of unfamiliar facts, foibles, and funny business about the famous. It covers (by which I mean uncovers) surprises about all kinds of bigwigs, and what you don't know just might astonish you.

When Kim Jong-un's father died, citizens who didn't know how to cry received instruction in weeping.

The film *Frankenpenis* is autobiographical.

The CIA considered causing Castro's iconic beard to fall out by covering his shoes with thallium, and Vladimir Putin was nominated for the 2014 Nobel Peace Prize.

Big names—small disclosures. Important historical data—little to none.

> Note: My own opinions are not necessarily nice. But I'm not out to tarnish my targets. My aim is to amuse, not to abuse.

Before dishing the dirt on household names, a housekeeping announcement. You've heard the term at conferences or concerts which begin with, "First, a few housekeeping details"—restroom location, phone etiquette, schedule minutiae, and maybe noting the auditorium EXIT signs.

And regarding exits, I'll weigh in too. This book is a shallow thing, for chapter-surfing and dipping into, not marathon swimming. Jump in anywhere. No need to start from the beginning and read straight through. Read a page or two while the kettle boils, or in the doctor's waiting room, or, if you're not a real bookworm, try moth mode. Flit around from page to page. Why stick slavishly to a text's actual sequence?

The samples I opened with demonstrate that the book includes people from a wide array of fields—sciences, technology, the arts, politics, society, economics, religion, philosophy, the military, plutocracy, fashion, crime, sports, medicine, and quackery. If there's any limit to the scope of the book, it's date.

My focus is on historic personages whose time-tested renown makes them household names. They're not only *historic*, however, but also *historical*. I omit many contemporary celebrities where I'm scooped—daily—by *People* magazine and other periodicals. *Today's* stars are grist for gossip too recent to get into the pages of a book.

Now two pieces of intro-info that are more material—namely disclaimers concerning authentication and attribution.

Authentication: About 1 percent of the data I provide is impossible to validate, as some of my characters lived up to centuries ago, with plenty of time in the interim for bits of hearsay to multiply like the heads of a Hydra. I suppose I could go through the motions of (futile) research into learned debates on this 1 percent, but as I've said, this book is as scholarly as a soapsud. It's as academic as air. You'll look in vain for a footnote.

Attribution: I don't as a rule cite sources, except where appropriate to credit an individual's work or opinions. Most of my facts are in the public domain and often anonymous anyway; you could ferret out these arcanum yourself if you had the interest or energy. My basic bibliography is my own purported brain. Nor need I acknowledge my research assistants, Google and Wikipedia, where I usually disregard any "citation needed" nonsense. In brief, I indemnify myself with this disclaimer and without taking legal advice.

Let's get to the substance of the book. Since they're exemplars of prominent people, we might as well begin with royalty. Their hereditary hold on the throne is literally grandfathered in. Obviously, monarchy is not the meritocracy one likes to see in any "ocracy," and most kings, queens, and emperors are nonentities, neither notable nor notorious.

You never know what you'll get in a sovereign who's the luck of the draw—in this case, DNA. In a gene pool, variety is a good thing. Inbreeding is not, and its result is iffy individuals. And in their iffiness lies their allure for us. Not all the royals I mention are *historic* figures, but in a few cases, their very wackiness warrants their presence here among the well-known.

I'll start with them but, as I said, *you* don't have to. *If you're not in the mood for monarchs, flip around through the pages. There are plenty of other Famous Freaks within.*

ROYALTY IN WESTERN HISTORY

The most important king to consider, of course, is *King Kong*. Hollywood named its gorilla "Kong" but then added the "King" because "Kong" alone sounded "too Chinese." They may not have known that in Chinese "Kong" means *hollow* or *empty*.

You might find Shakespeare's *Henry IV* of lesser artistic merit than *King Kong*, but notice another reference to a "hollow crown":

> For God's sake, let us sit upon the ground And tell
> sad stories of the death of kings . . . All murder'd:
> *for within the hollow crown That rounds the mortal*
> *temples of a king* Keeps Death his court and there the
> antic sits . . . Comes at the last and with a little pin
> Bores through his castle wall, and farewell king!

And in Shakespeare's *Richard II,* once again the vulnerability motif: "Uneasy lies the head that wears a crown." Or, as Frederick the Great of Prussia put it, "A crown is merely a hat that lets the rain in."

Henry IV might bemoan the "death of kings," but a feature of monarchy is its automatic handover when a ruler dies, saving the voter a trip to the polls. *Le roi est mort, vive le roi.* And for the peasant in the potato field, sovereigns were indistinguishable from one another, so a royal death made little difference.

Besides, a son often inherits his father's given name. To differentiate same-name monarchs, their nicknames highlighted their

1

individual traits. Take France. We have *Louis the Lazy, Louis the Stammerer, Louis the Frightened, Louis the Debonair,* and, piquantly, *Louis the Universal Spider* (Louis XI's sobriquet reflecting his webs of intrigue). *Louis XIV* called himself the *Sun King*; as god's deputy on earth, he was the center of the solar system.

Then you have your French Charleses: *the Bald, the Fat, the Simple, the Affable, the Mad.* And *The Great, a.k.a. Charlemagne.*

Charlemagne (b. 748)

The territory Charlemagne conquered was the largest since the Roman Empire, and due to this fact, some dub him the "Father of Europe" (and there will be a few more "Fathers" of this or that before this book is done).

A fact too odd to be false: When nobles appeared before Charlemagne dressed in their party silks, he took them out to hunt and afterwards ridiculed them for their wrecked attire. This sounds a little mean, but a couple of things make him more endearing.

Charlemagne tried hard to learn how to write—secretly, on tablets hidden under his pillow. He failed. Ironically, however, he standardized the script *Carolingian miniscule* (named for him) which introduced two new concepts: spaces between words and upper- and lower-case lettering.

His envoy, Isaac the Jew, brought him a present from Caliph Harun al-Rashid—Charlemagne's greatly-beloved elephant Abul Abbas. Eighteenth-century fishermen found several of its bones.

Charlemagne was a man of physical as well as political stature. Specialists dug up Charlemagne's remains in 1861; in 2010, X-rays and a CT scan of his leg bone indicated he was six feet tall. He obviously outstripped his father Pepin the Short and probably his son Pepin the Hunchback.

At his coronation, the Pope startled Charlemagne by crowning him not king but emperor. From Charlemagne's Latin name, *Carolus*, several European countries derive their word for "king": *król* in Poland; король in Russia; *král* in Czechoslovakia and Turkey, and *Király* in Hungary, which is the root of the *cyrillic* Slavic alphabet.

Charles the Mad, initially *Charles the Beloved* (b. 1368)
Since Charles VI thought he was made of glass, he padded his clothes to prevent himself from shattering. This book is supposed to discuss household names, but let's give the fragile Charles an honorary entry.

Frederick Barbarossa; "red-bearded" (b. 1122)
It was unwise to mess with Barbarossa's wife. A report from the seventeenth-century historian Nathaniel Wanley (*Wonders of the Little World*) tells us how, when his enemies humiliated his wife by making her sit backwards on a mule, Frederick allowed them to live provided they "with their teeth, take a fig out of the genitals of a mule." The punishment certainly fit the crime.

Scandinavian Kings

If you had to choose, though it's just as well you don't, which of these Danish royals would you want as your sovereign?

Harald Bluetooth, whom you would know as ᚼᛅᚱᛅᛚᛏᚱ ᛬ ᛒᛚᛏᚢᚦᛆ
Sweyne Forkbeard
Sigrid the Haughty
Thorbjorg Knarrarbringa ("Boat-size Breasts"), mother of Eric the Red
Harald Harefoot
Olaf Hunger
Folke the Fat
Ivar the Boneless
Eric II the Memorable, though not remembered fondly
Eric (XI) the Lisper and Lame
Hafr-Bjǫrn (i.e., Billy-goat), who had a vision of owning profitable goats
Or perhaps—

Canute (Knut); Viking; King of Denmark, Norway, and England (b. 994)

Canute is said to have boasted that he could command the tide not to come in—another report too weird to be false. But the actual fact is that he was showing his subjects that it wouldn't work, since no one was greater than God.

His wife was *Ælfgifu* ("elves' gift"). According to the Social Security Administration, who keeps baby-name statistics, "This name is not popular in the US, as there are no popularity data for the name." With this name's lack of popularity, Canute's Ælfgifu, incidentally, may be the mysterious mistress of a priest in one panel of the Bayeux Tapestry.

Prussia

Frederick the Great; "Old Fritz"; Prussian king; and Pennsylvania town (b. 1712)
The town King of Prussia (known for its massive mall, the US's third biggest) was named as a tribute to Frederick's opposition to the British. There are worse place names, but not many.

Frederick founded the *Potsdam Giants* regiment, seeking to propagate giants by marrying its men to tall women. Darwin himself later credits this early attempt at genetic manipulation:

> Nor have certain male and female individuals been intentionally picked out and matched, except in the well-known case of the of the Prussian grenadiers; and in this case man obeyed, as might have been expected, the law of methodical selection . . .

Russia

Ivan The Terrible (Ивáн Грóзный); *Ivan IV* (b. 1540)
Sky History writes: "The seeds of the dreadful human being Ivan would become were sewn [sic] in his miserable childhood," a case of behavior modification by a royal seamstress. Whether you blame nature or nurture, Ivan shows us what atrocities a human being is capable of.

After building Moscow's St. Basil's Cathedral, he reportedly ordered that its designer be blinded to keep him from building a competing church for anyone else.

Ivan bound citizens of Novgorod to sleighs which he shoved into a half-frozen river; oarsmen pushed any survivors back under the ice. *Boyars* (landed nobles) and middle-class families were literally grilled for information, their eyebrows burned off and their bodies scorched. As for subjects who didn't hail him as divine, he boiled them alive. (He murdered up to six hundred people daily.)

He battered his son's pregnant wife because he judged her clothes indecent. When his son objected, Ivan killed him with a sharpened stick.

His bones, exhumed in 1963, showed mercury poisoning from a skin salve.

Peter the Great (b. 1672)
When he was ten, he became co-tsar—but not co-star, since his older siblings ran the show. His most admirable feat was attaining a height of six feet eight inches; his most horrific deeds included torture and the murder of thousands.

Empress Anna Ivanovna, daughter of *Ivan the Ignorant* (b. 1693)
The nineteenth-century Scottish writer Thomas Carlyle compares her famous enlarged cheek to a "Westphalian ham," and a portrait corroborates his opinion.

Her marriage was an ill-fated union. Czar Peter the Great's biographer Lindsey Hughes tells how he mocked her marriage with a public spectacle featuring a wedding of two dwarfs. In a drinking competition with the Czar, the new husband drank too much and died of alcohol poisoning eight weeks after the wedding.

During her reign, Russian Prince Mikhaíl committed the outrage of marrying a Roman Catholic. When this heathen wife died, Anna punished the Prince by appointing him court jester. His job description was to mimic a hen laying eggs. We begin to dislike this woman.

Anna was vindictive and then some. Not to mention her sick sense of humor, if we want to call it that. She made the widowed prince marry an ugly housemaid. And she added injury to insult: The wedding pair had to wear clown suits and ride an elephant. As further torment, she commissioned a roomy ice palace, dimensions thirty-three feet by eighty feet. Bed, seats, stairs, plus the fireplace and its logs—were made of ice. She imprisoned them there for their wedding night; less than a week later, the bride died.

Catherine the Great (b. 1729)
If for your whole life you've been thinking she was fatally trampled by a horse during an act of bestiality, forget it. A routine stroke killed her.

Mind you, I'm not saying the bestiality is a lie.

Britain

William the Conqueror, a.k.a. *William the Bastard* (b. 1028)
Unlike Empress Anna's jester, William's fool played catalyst in a major political event in 1066: the Norman Conquest. The murder of this fool triggered the opening attack in in the Battle of Hastings, where William won the English throne after King Harold, the Anglo-Saxon incumbent, was shot in the eye. Harold's mother was willing to pay (to William) Harold's weight in gold for the return of his body, but William denied the request and instead cut up the corpse.

But he wasn't all bad. He got rid of the death penalty, changing the sentence to blinding and castration.

People mocked him for his obesity, saying he looked pregnant; he went to a French spa for a special herbal diet.

Later, after he was thrown from his horse, his intestines ruptured, and he died of sepsis. His body was so swollen that when they tried to cram him into his coffin he exploded. His vassals left him on the floor and made off with plenty of his belongings.

From the continent William brought (via French) 50 percent of our English language, without which we'd be speaking some strange consonant-throttled Anglo-Saxon.

Richard Lionheart (b. 1157)
Richard was as good as William was nasty. For a start, he knighted his chef as "Lord of the Fief of the Kitchen of the Counts of Poitou."

Jews had been barred from Richard's coronation, but they attended anyway; they were ejected with their clothes torn off. Richard, on the other hand, subsequently forbade persecution of Jews.

As he lay dying of gangrene from a crossbow wound, he ordered the guilty French archer hanged. But when he learned his killer was a mere boy (using a frying-skillet as a shield), he pardoned him and handed him 100 shillings. After Richard died, however, his chief officer had the boy flayed alive before being hanged.

An alternative story that is too dull an option for us has Richard dying of starvation in an English castle after Henry IV usurped his throne. Feel free to consider either tale apocryphal. I'm going with the boy and arrow, per my usual rule that peculiar details are the most plausible. Academic note: translators of ancient texts agree with me. Their fancy term for the principle is *lectio difficilior*—the least-expected wording is the correct one.

Henry VIII (b. 1491)

As we know from Holbein's portrait, he was fat. His armor reveals a fifty-four-inch waist, and he weighed in at close to four hundred pounds.

He divorced Catherine of Aragon, the first of his six wives, despite the Catholic prohibition. He conveniently created his own substitute religion; the Church of England remains the state religion, which is the basic Roman creed minus the Pope.

Elizabeth I (b. 1533)

Like Richard Lionheart, Elizabeth was generous to underlings. According to the *Annotated Mother Goose* (William and Ceil Baring-Gould), an old rhyme told how she gave a diamond to a visiting child. Another British nursery rhyme, by the way—totally unrelated to Queen Elizabeth—was used by a twentieth-century American performer: Jazz king Nathaniel Adams assumed the name *Nat King Cole* in honor of "Old King Cole."

Queen Victoria (b. 1819)
As for Victoria, the principal thing to know is that *Victoria's Secret* was named after her to evoke the elegance of the Victorian era. The "secret" part refers to what lies under the lingerie.

Edward VIII, Edward Albert Christian George Andrew Patrick David, King of the United Kingdom and the Dominions of the British Empire, and Emperor of India (b. 1894)
I wouldn't apply for a position with a royal job description. Nor should Edward have done so. His father George V said, "After I am dead, the boy will ruin himself in twelve months."

He did indeed end up abdicating to marry Wallis Simpson. But if she was his ruin, I blame only her given names. Hard to say which name is worse for a queen, Wallis or Bessie.

Spain: Two Certifiable Wack Jobs

Joanna the Mad (Juana la Loca) of Castille (b. 1479)
Royal madness again. It's all over the place, partially the result of inbreeding where marital options were few. You paint yourself into a genetic corner when you're at the aristocratic apex and not allowed to marry beneath yourself.

In 1496, Joanna's marriage was arranged to Philip the Handsome, Austrian archduke. When he died, her son Charles V, not trusting her political stance, locked her up as a madwoman, giving himself free rein to reign.

Modern medicine diagnoses possible depression or genetic schizophrenia (based on her paranoia nuns plotting her murder). To eat, sleep, or care for herself Joanna allegedly depended on caregivers. Charles prohibited visitors—maybe for fear they'd find her sane. On the other hand, on a royal tour the ambassador of Venice declared Joanna "a wise queen."

Charles the Bewitched (El Hechizado); Carlos II (b. 1661)
Carlos slept with his father's exhumed body—a treatment prescribed to help him sire a royal son.

Carlos's post-mortem showed his "heart was the size of a peppercorn; his lungs corroded; his intestines rotten and gangrenous; he had a single testicle [atrophied], black as coal, and his head was full of water."

German Professor VanKerrebroeck puts this in simpler terms: "We can conclude that Carlos suffered from posterior hypospadias, monarchism and an atrophic testicle. He probably had an intersexual state with ambiguous genitalia, and a congenital monokidney with stones and infections."

Additional medical notes:

I'm not violating Carlos's HIPAA patient confidentiality rights; according to the BMJ neurology journal, "The patient has provided written consent, which can be obtained on request by the editor." Good to know. From the journal:

What with his health issues, it's not surprising that Carlos II was the end of the Habsburg line. Carlos "suffered from a range of ailments extending beyond the well-known Habsburg jaw, including developmental delay, intellectual disability, dysarthria, skeletal deformity, recurrent infections, epilepsy and infertility." He had "a large tongue, plump, round lips, a cupid bow upper lip, a flat, broad nose and large forehead . . . near continuous drooling."

We mustn't assume, however, that he was stupid. He was under the tutelage of Mariana Engracia Álvarez de Toledo Portugal y Alfonso-Pimentel, governess to kings, and if nothing else her name alone suggests her stature.

Inbreeding was the rule in the Habsburg dynasty, beginning with a certain Guntram the Rich (tenth century) and Radbot, who was not a fantasy-game villain but Guntram's grandson. I could detail the Spanish seventeenth-century "blood purity" law *limpieza* de *sangre*; I could, *if* I could, explain the coefficient of inbreeding (F) cited in the BMJ paper for genetic risk among "heterozygote carriers of the aspartylglucosaminuria in different members of the family."

ANCIENT KINGS

King David (ninth century BCE)

Everyone knows David killed Goliath the Philistine.

Detailed recap: David's brother Eliab craved the glory of slaying Goliath. David was a puny shepherd, and when he showed up on the scene, Eliab slanged him about leaving his sheep unattended: "I know thy pride," said Eliab, "and the naughtiness of thine heart; for thou art come down that thou mightest see the battle." Well, Eliab was about to learn a thing or two about slanging.

David couldn't let the insult pass without responding. He did at least have pasture cred, and he pointed out unto King Saul that when "there came a lion, and a bear, and took a lamb out of the flock . . . I smote him and delivered it out of his mouth."

Still, David deemed himself unworthy of the honor of wearing armor, so he "chose him five smooth stones . . . and his sling was in his hand."

Naturally Goliath "disdained him: for he was but a youth," and warned him, "I will give thy flesh unto the fowls of the air, and to the beasts of the field," these two classes of vertebrate being a recurrent motif in the Bible. And David took a stone "and slang it, and smote the Philistine . . . the stone sunk into his forehead; and he fell upon his face to the earth."

David, however, also has a less honorable homicide to his credit. To avoid the adverse optics of a direct murder, he sent Uriah the Hittite, the husband of his mistress, Bathsheba, into battle, secretly telling the commanders to put him into the front line where he was sure to be killed.

By the way, scholars now deny that David wrote the *Psalms of David*.

Sennacherib—pronunciation aid: the neo-Assyrian cuneiform is ⸰⊣ 𒀀⸰⊣ ⊢⸰ ⸱𒌍 (reign 705-681 BCE)
Even if his name doesn't ring a bell, I hope it will henceforth. He richly deserves his place here.

His name means "Sîn has replaced the brothers," but note the subtle circumflex, indicating that Sîn is a nickname for "Sennacherib".

Even meaning "sin," the name might have been appropriate. The Assyrians thought Sennacherib's soldiers were incarnations of Gog and Magog, which we recall are two nations allied with Satan. Sennacherib gloats:

> Terror of doing battle with me overwhelmed them like alû-demons. They abandoned their tents and passed their urine hotly, (and) released their excrement inside their chariots.

And no wonder. According to *Dungeons and Dragons*: an "Alu-Demon has the compound, bug-like eyes of the Chasme. The more mundane Alu-Demons are sometimes mistaken for Tieflings. Other demonic traits include sharpened claws; an exterior skull (particularly unsettling); gray, black, or green skin; ram horns; boney protrusions; or a leathery tail.

In the palace in Ninevah, Sennacherib's wife was homesick for her lush motherland Media (the region, not communications channels), so he fashioned The Hanging Gardens of Babylon, one of the official Seven Wonders of the Ancient World. Except that—although five ancient writers attest to Sennacherib as its designer—

Nebuchadnezzar usually gets the credit. Descriptions dwell on the advanced engineering that irrigated lofty trees growing on a series of balconies.

Nebuchadnezzar II—𒀭𒉿𒆪𒁺𒌨𒊑 to his associates (reign 605–562 BCE)
Nebuchadnezzar had a checkered record. After the destruction of the First Temple, he banished the Jews from Judah: their Babylonian Captivity lasted sixty years. Psalm 137 shows the cruel commands they were given:

> By the rivers of Babylon, there we sat down, yea, we wept, when we remembered Zion. We hanged our harps upon the willows in the midst thereof. For there they that carried us away captive required of us a song; and they that wasted us required of us mirth, saying, sing us one of the songs of Zion. How shall we sing the Lord's song in a strange land?

Nebuchadnezzar asked a crew of "magicians, enchanters, sorcerers and astrologers" to interpret one of his dreams, adding that if they didn't oblige, he would "have you cut into pieces and your houses turned into piles of rubble." Luckily one of these men, Daniel, secured amnesty for them as well as explaining the dream.

When three of Daniel's friends—Shadrach, Meschach, and Abednego—refused, Nebuchadnezzar had them thrown into a fiery furnace—though he had second thoughts when he noticed his victims walking around unharmed in the fire. *Oho*, the king probably said to himself, *I detect some kind of divine agency at work here. I might want to rescue these folks.*

King Xerxes the Great (reign 486–465 BCE)
When a storm wrecked a flimsy bridge across the Hellespont, the Persian king Xerxes commanded his men to give the water three-hundred lashes—and drop chains into the strait for good measure. The bridge builders were put to death, and if you build a bridge out of papyrus, what do you expect?

History is muddy on the various Xerxeses. The book of Esther describes a Xerxes (this one better known as Ahasuerus) who was very taken with a certain Esther. He promised her whatever she wished for, "it shall be even given thee to the half of the kingdom." Esther asks him to just stop killing the Jews.

To shoehorn in a note on the wish theme: Fairy tales and myths are full of power figures making this kind of rash pledge. It's a good plot device. Take the goddess Eos (on behalf of Tithonus), and the Cumaean Sibyl (on behalf of herself), who both made a request that backfired: eternal life, but they forgot the part about eternal youth. Another who messed up was Semele, who insisted on viewing Zeus in his true godlike persona—a sight a mortal can see only when dead. And Zeus had kept his promise, so that was the end of Semele until Handel revived her in an opera.

But back to the Esther and Xerxes/Ahasuerus. According to one midrash, he ordered his wife Vashti to dance naked for his guests. When she refused, they naturally assumed that her unclothed body was disfigured by leprosy (which was stupid, since leprosy notably attacks the visible extremities) or—more interesting—that she had a tail. This hypothesis was also stupid, unless you believe one scholar's hypothesis that the tail was a phallus, and she was either hermaphroditic or transgender.

Cleopatra (b. 69 BCE)
Royal incest again? Her parents may have been siblings. Although Cleopatra herself "married" her own younger brothers, those

marriages were titular, not physical. Some other facts about Cleopatra: Since Caesar was a political enemy, she once had hidden in a sack to sneak into his house. In the 1963 movie *Cleopatra*, Elizabeth Taylor's wardrobe cost $200,000, which in 2023 would be $1.9 million.

Cleopatra's main contribution to us is some beauty tips. For example, available now from Premier Cosmetics is *Dead Sea Salt Mask* ($50/5 oz.): "Attain Cleopatra's Glow." Better yet, *Cleopatra Blend* from Gritman—"Female-oriented towards sexual strength and male attraction." She is said to have allegedly bathed in donkey milk.

About Cleopatra's nose, the French writer Pascal says: S*i le nez de Cléopâtre eût été plus court, toute la face du monde aurait changé.* In other words, her beauty changed the course of world history.

The historian Plutarch describes how Cleopatra staged a striking mise-en-scène expressly to wow the Roman triumvir, Antony. And Shakespeare corroborates Plutarch's precise details:

> The barge she sat in, like a burnish'd throne,
> Burned on the water: the poop was beaten gold;
> Purple the sails, and so perfumed that
> The winds were lovesick with them; the oars were silver,
> Which to the tune of flutes kept stroke, and made
> The water which they beat to follow faster,
> As amorous of their strokes. For her own person,
> It beggar'd all description: she did lie
> In her pavilion, cloth-of-gold of tissue . . .

Plutarch denies the legend of Cleopatra's suicide by asp, but some modern research posits that she wore a barrette soaked in fatal venom.

Alexander the Great (b. 356 BCE)

One of his teachers mentioned his red-gold hair. Maybe. But I bet that teacher was accurate in the odder item of his eyes—one blue, one brown.

Nor do I doubt he was afraid of cats because who would make it up.

Alexander named at least seventy cities after himself.

He gave another conquered town the name of his horse, Bucephalus. His father had refused the horse for himself as too ornery, but Alexander predicted that its skittishness was fear of its own shadow and tamed the unruly animal, as befits a hero—even a scaredy-cat with respect to cats.

Alexander ran into the philosopher Diogenes, the Cynic known for walking around with a lamp in broad daylight "looking for an honest man." Diogenes lived, naked, in a big clay jar. When Alexander enquired what gift he'd like, Diogenes asked him with more candor than courtesy to move away and stop blocking the sun—a modest request compared to those I touched on a couple of pages ago, namely eternal life.

If you like a "stylistic mixture of progressive rock and metal," perhaps you know the band Gordian Knot. But if you haven't heard of the original Gordian Knot, you should have. No one but a great emperor could untie it. When Alexander failed, he took his sword and snipped the knotted rope. I call this unacceptable cheating; consider how the young King Arthur pulled Excalibur from the rock with honest elbow grease.

Alexander obviously hankered after imperial prestige, and he ordered the conquered Persians to prostrate themselves before him. He gave up the idea when they just laughed at him. We see this prostration requirement through many centuries and cultures, and we can only hope that not many of the rulers' subjects suffered from insubordination or arthritis.

Alexander also had problems with anger management, particularly when drunk. Example: during a party given for a friend, Alexander killed the guest of honor.

He himself died when he was thirty-two.

A Primer on Sub-Royal Nobility and Selected Titled Individuals

Monarchs are only the acme of a vast aristocratic organization chart. I'll begin with two pieces of floury aristocratic etymology on the off chance you're interested.

The title *aristocrat* is derived from Greek *aristos*, "best," the term for the tasseled top of the wheat stalk which contains the grain.

The word *lord* started life as *hlāfweard* "loaf-ward"—bread—guardian.

And before listing various peculiarities of individual patricians, let's review three systems of metrics which highlight the awareness of rank that pervades our culture.

Aristocratic Terms of Measure
For your reference, here's a lot more than you need to know about dimensions of slate roof tiles:

- Empress (26x18 inches)
- Wide Duchess (61.0 x 35.6)
- Wide Viscountess (45.7 x 25.4)
- Broad Lady (16 x 9)
- Small Lady (14 x 8)
- Narrow Lady (14 x 7)

Liquid measures:

- Jeroboam (3 liters)
- Rehoboam (4.5-liters), tenth-century BC king of Judah
- Methuselah (6 liters), who as we know lived 969 years
- Salmanazar (9 liters), Assyrian king
- Balthazar (12 liters), Arabian king, one of the three Magi
- Nebuchadnezzar, our Babylonian friend (15 liters, weight 83 lbs.)
- Solomon (18 liters), very *recherché* size, exclusively French
- Sovereign (25 liters, equivalent of 34 bottles)
- Melchizedek (30 liters = 240 glasses). Some say it doesn't actually exist.

On more familiar territory than roofing or bubbly, there's the mattress. Mattress sizes include the Queen, the King, and the California King, which is a stupid name, because the only royalty on the west coast is the Alaska King crab which is more arthropod than aristocrat and not what you're looking for in a bed. The *International Sleep Product Association* explains that the California size was invented in Los Angeles to reflect Hollywood stars' lifestyle.

In bed sizes, you also have your Eastern Kings, not to be confused with the Three Kings as in Magi. But it's people who are our topic, so let's leave the bewildering mattress nomenclature behind and return to human beings and their titles, from emperor down to the paltry peerage.

Emperor

The Emperors' main job was as arbiters of fashion. There's the *imperial* look, usually a small, pointed beard growing below the lower lip, popular during the Empire of Napoleon III.

We all know everything about the "emperor's new clothes," because there's *nothing* to know.

Extant today is the "empire" style in women's dresses. In the 1700s, European fashion favored Classical culture in furniture, architecture, art, and attire. As seen mainly in Jane Austen movies, an empire-style gown had no waist; it was cinched under the bosom and fell from there to the ankle. Napoleon's wife Josephine was much given to the style, particularly handy for a pregnant empress.

While the look lasted, it was a happy holiday from corsets. But in the dialectics of fashion, comfort gave way again to the hourglass figure—tight-laced whalebone stays and bustles. The corsets constricted the lungs, which is why women were always fainting.

Beyond fashion trends, we can't forget *imperial measure*, named in the heyday of the British empire, which rejected the decimal system for an "imperial" version based on inches (1 inch = 3 barleycorns), feet, yards, stone, chains, furlongs, and miles. Liquids are measured in pecks, gallons, quarts, pints, gills, and ounces. Weights include ounces, pounds avoirdupois, and cental hundredweights. By the way, the abbreviation lb. for pounds derives from *libra pondo*, where *libra* = "scales" (as in the astrological sign) and *pondo* = "weight," as in "ponderous."

Tsar

Spelled *czar*, it shows its derivation from *caesar*, as does the German *kaiser*.

A tsar is basically an emperor.

Prince

The first thing to know is their place in the hierarchy of angel choirs. At the top, of course, you have your Seraphim and Cherubim, followed (depending how you list the chain of command) by Thrones, Dominions, Virtues, Powers, and lowly Princedoms.

Archangels and Angels report directly to Princedoms, who manage earthly affairs and look like blobs of light; team co-leaders are Netzach and Hamiel. Lacking access to confidential personnel files, that's all I can tell you. As for our own singer-songwriter Prince, including his real identity, see his details below.

Marquis/Marquess/Margrave

I'd like to be a "margrave." The title has a *je ne sais quoi* of gravitas.

A *marquise diamond* (58 facets) is cut to copy the shape of the mouth of Madame de Pompadour, Louis XV's mistress. Choose it as a change from the more common (square) *princess* cut.

A *marquee* (from marquis, seventeenth century) was initially the fancy roof on the tents of military officers—a sign of their superior rank. It became any *ad hoc* canopy and from there a theatre entrance.

Duke and Duchess

An odd expression: *Put up your dukes*, hence *duke it out*. Its origin is Cockney rhyming slang, which involves words with long and non-intuitive verbal chains back to something crazily unrelated. "Dukes" is an example: fingers/hands were nicknamed "forks," which evolved into the rhyming "Duke of Yorks," whence fists became "dukes."

For some Baby Boomers, the word *duke* will conjure up the 1962 rock hit *Duke of Earl*, an irritating title that defies logic. The name originated with The Dukays, a vocal group out of Chicago. (Reasoning for the name: a member of the group was named Earl.)

But *The* Duke, of course, is Marion Robert Morrison, also known as John Wayne. He picked up the nickname from his childhood dog "Duke." Hollywood was not having any male star named Marion. To suggest a tough guy, Fox Studios first came up with Anthony Wayne, the American Revolution general. Another Fox VIP, however, balked at the Italian-sounding "Anthony," no good for a red-blooded all-American 1950s screen icon. The same xenophobia we saw with "Kong."

Toughness brings us to the unattractive *Duchess* in *Alice in Wonderland*. One rumor is that Lewis Carroll and the illustrator John Tenniel modelled her after a sixteenth-century painting, "The Ugly Duchess," who is in turn rumored to be Margaret, Countess of Tyrol (known more graphically as "bag-mouth" and allegedly the ugliest woman the world had ever known, with the dubious honor of outranking even the Westphalian Ham described above).

Alice in Wonderland was once banned in parts of China. "Bears, lions, and other beasts cannot use human language," said the Governor of the Hunan Province in 1931. "To attribute to them such a power is an insult to the human race."

Earl
Earl Grey Tea honors Charles, the second Earl Grey, a Prime Minister in the 1830s. Earl Grey is black tea instilled with *bergamot* (Ottoman, "the Master's Pear").

Another noble notable in the gustatory field was the fourth *Earl of Sandwich*. He created a convenient sandwich to avoid missing one instant of betting at the gambling table.

Count
Mid-level management.

Voivode
You find this originally military rank in Eastern Europe, where *voi* is a cognate word of English *war*. To us the title is obscure, by which I mean unheard-of. But I include it for two important reasons.

First, it's a silly-sounding word—not that I know how to pronounce it.

Secondly, it's the title/rank of the charismatic *Voivode of Wallachia*, national Romanian hero and villain, whom we know as *Count Dracula* or *Vlad III*, cognomen *Vlad the Impaler* (circa 1428-1477).

A papal ambassador provides our sole physical description of the real Vlad: shortish, stoutly built, with a narrow ruddy face, swollen nostrils and temples, large green eyes, heavy dark eyebrows, and a thick neck covered by black curls.

Out of paranoia, he assassinated a number of *boyars*. These were the same threatening landed gentry and bourgeoisie whom Ivan the Terrible would slaughter in the following century. Vlad also impaled whole families of Transylvanian Saxons; witnesses listed precise dates of the atrocity. Scholars Florescu & McNally (*In Search of Dracula*) claim the Transylvanians called him a "demented psychopath, a sadist, a gruesome murderer, and masochist," and they were not overstating the case.

Vlad was a man of many monstrous talents. He devised a massive cauldron and covered it with a top pierced with holes for the heads of persons inserted in the boiling water below.

Disclaimer: I repeat these horrific tales less out of ghoulishness than because I'm supposed to be listing outré facts. It's true that some Vlad stories are almost too horrific to be false: he had nursing women speared, then sliced off their breasts, which he impaled on the same stakes as their babies.

In another account, Vlad skewered a pair of monks (to "help them get to heaven," an act of Christian charity), then impaled their donkey for braying to mourn its masters.

When a few visiting emissaries from Turkey declined to remove their turbans, Vlad fixed the turbans to their heads with spikes. A good lesson on *lèse-majesté*.

In the fifteenth century, Gabriele Rangoni claimed that during his imprisonment, lacking for better prey, Vlad sliced up rats and stuck them on small pieces of wood. Bad habits die hard.

But never mind these shenanigans. The king of Hungary knighted him as Count in the *Order of the Dragon*. It was not until then (1431) that Vlad got the deceptively sweet name "Dracula" ("little dragon") and the title voivode: *Dracula vodă* (Count Dracula).

Bram Stoker's 1897 novel *Dracula*, added vampirism to the Count's vices.

Vlad stories were contemporary hits, thanks to new printing technology showing graphic brutality, such as woodcuts (circa 1500) of Vlad dining with a background of victims being tortured on stakes.

Actor Bela Lugosi played Dracula in two films: *Dracula* and *Abbott and Costello Meet Frankenstein*. The Library of Congress classed the latter as "culturally, historically, or aesthetically significant."

TYRANTS AND DICTATORS

Mao Zedong; Chairman Mao (b. 1893)

Mao's executions and imposed labor killed tens of millions of Chinese citizens. His industrialization program *Great Leap Forward* triggered starvation, where some people reportedly even resorted to cannibalism. The regime, however, forbade designating "starvation" as an official cause of death.

Mao was detail oriented. For instance, he instituted an insect bounty in which citizens were paid for corpses of flies and mosquitoes (also rats and sparrows).

He had peculiar personal health and hygiene habits. When the doctor told him to quit cigarettes, Mao quipped, "Smoking is also a deep-breathing exercise." Good point.

In dental care, Mao shunned the toothbrush. He used tea as mouthwash and munched tea leaves. When the doctor, noting the rotten teeth, criticized this practice, Mao came back with: "Does a tiger brush his teeth?" He used the same metaphor again, comparing Russian treatment of China to "taking meat from the mouth of a tiger."

The Chairman refused to have his persistent STD treated.

Less quaintly, his wife got rid of his chronic constipation manually. Think about it. Or better yet, don't.

Even with Mao and statecraft, we seem to be stuck in excreta. A Russian spy claimed Stalin sought a sample of Mao's feces for personality analysis—a time-honored practice use by the ancient Greeks for *scatomancy.*

Mao held a conference in a pool to humiliate Khrushchev, knowing the latter could not swim and would need water wings.

Because they were a drag on his economy, Mao wanted the US to admit as residents ten million Chinese women.

Charles Manson only wished for it, but Mao actually *is* displayed in a glass (crystal) coffin in Tiananmen Square.

Pol Pot (b. 1925)

A funny name for a non-funny individual. The name means "the original Cambodian," but it wasn't original for him since he was born *Saloth Sar*.

Pol Pot was chronically ill with malaria, GI ills, and serious insomnia.

Peculiar predilection: He liked French poems, and he liked Verlaine best. (French was an official government language in Indochina until 1953.)

Many other facts about this ruler are well-known, but I'll mention them anyway to flesh out his profile.

As "Prime Minister," Pol Pot micro-ruled Cambodia from 1975–79, his "Reign of Terror."

He moved the entire urban population—and with them all the skilled labor the economy had been depending on—to collective farms. He controlled how they dressed (black clothes only), their sex lives, and their language. He banned money, religion, and virtually all books. He emptied schools and drafted children into the army. His military arm, the Khmer Rouge (namely Communists), rearranged rice fields into a precise checked pattern. The imposed collective farming caused widespread famine.

In the notorious Killing Fields, the Khmer Rouge executed any suspected political opponents and any minority, which included intellectuals and anyone who presumed to wear a watch or glasses.

Between 1.5 and 2 million—25 percent of Cambodians—were murdered, mostly with pickaxes.

Kim Jong-un (b. 1984)
The twenty-seven-year-old Kim Jong-un came to power in 2019 as Supreme Leader of North Korea, and unless you count Donald Trump's favorable opinion ("We fell in love"), there's not much to recommend him.

Under Kim Jong-un the country takes respect for its leader seriously:

- When his father died, citizens who didn't know how to cry were instructed in how to weep, and smiling is banned on July 8, the date of his death.
- Each household has a duster dedicated to cleaning the Leader's portrait.
- You can't get married on Kim's birthday.
- A man was executed for falling asleep during one of his speeches.

Other taboos:

- International telephone calls are a criminal offense.
- You need a permit to use electricity, which is cut off at night due to low supply.
- Jeans are illegal.
- As recently as 2020, Kim banned dogs in Pyongyang—these pets represented Western "decadence." Rumors circulated that they would be ground up into meat for starving North Koreans.
- You can be executed for watching an American movie (for an Indian film, it's only jail).

- On the one hand, you cannot leave the country (border guards shoot you if you try); on the other hand, you need a special license to live in the capital city.

All the way down to your grandchildren, your family can be penalized for your crimes. Although the Bible, part of Western culture, is banned, the Kim family had clearly taken a leaf out of the Book of Deuteronomy: "I the LORD thy God am a jealous God, visiting the iniquity of the fathers upon the children unto the third and fourth generation of them that hate me."

In 2016 some Chinese citizens were calling him 金三胖—"Fatty the Third," until China officially banned the name. You don't mess with a foreign leader like Pol Pot.

Kim apparently favors elevator shoes to add to his stature. At five feet, three inches, he has at times weighed up to three hundred pounds. Some blamed this high figure (and his figure) on his partiality to Swiss cheese, for which his country spent annually thousands of dollars, dwarfed only by his annual personal champagne budget of $30 million. When Covid stopped imports, he lost about forty-five pounds.

His obesity notwithstanding, this boy man really cares about his appearance: He had cosmetic surgery to increase his resemblance to his grandfather. Other than this ancestor, however, Kim must have no equal. If your name is Kim, you have to change it. No one is allowed to copy his personal flat-top hairstyle. Males have a choice of ten haircuts. (A woman's coiffure must be on a list of only eighteen legal styles. Once a woman marries, she has to cut her hair shorter.)

It's not astonishing to hear that his car is a Maybach, a car too elite for many of us to have heard of. When he's asea, he's on his $8-million yacht staffed by the twenty-four servants whom he'll need on his own party island, where "party" is not socialist but social.

He possesses his own train (in two senses: his personal retinue and his personal railroad).

This boy failed every school exam. He still finds video games more fun than intellectual challenges. He's a basketball devotee, particularly partial to the Chicago Bulls and the Los Angeles Lakers. The lucky Supreme Leader can indulge in Western culture denied to a lower class of person.

This lifestyle entails some collateral damage, by which I mean (for one) the murder of his brother by girl goons with the nerve agent VX.

Depending on your politics, you might say Kim Jong-un had a single flash of sanity when he called Donald Trump "a mentally deranged US dotard." Except for the dotard part, you could also say it takes one to know one. Evidently the mutual love described by Trump was elusive.

American student Otto Warmbier was arrested in 2017 for stealing a poster at his hotel; he fell ill, came home, and died—presumably from maltreatment or outright torture.

Idi Amin Dada Oumee; His Excellency President for Life; Field Marshal Al Hadji Doctor Idi Amin, VC, DSO, MC, CBE; Lord of all the Beasts of the Earth and Fishes of the Sea, and Conqueror of the British Empire in Africa in General and Uganda in Particular; a.k.a. president of Uganda (b. 1925)

And considering a title like that, what more is there to say? Unfortunately, there is more to say.

One of Idi Amin's wives, "Suicide Sarah," belonged to the Revolutionary Suicide Mechanised Regiment Band; a former go-go dancer, she became a hairdresser after the marriage. Best man at their wedding: Yasser Arafat, leader of the Palestine Liberation Organization.

Idi Amin fathered about sixty children.

He started his career as the Ugandan boxing champion. Moving up from sparring to slaughter, he would oversee the murders of three hundred thousand Ugandans. Example of his *modus operandi*: in 1996, when Kenyans in Uganda supported Israel, he executed 245 of them.

But that piece of brutality is well known—other instances maybe less so. In his palace, Idi Amin built a torture chamber. His specifications included five subsections. It was here that two-thirds of his victims reportedly succumbed. An electric fence surrounded the building, and for another level of security water in its hallways caused electrocution. It's reported he had handicapped citizens thrown to the crocodiles in the Nile.

Henry Kayenba's biography alludes to the postmortem removal of his victims' livers, kidneys, lips, and genitals. Amin is even alleged to have stored people's heads in his fridge. He reportedly liked to boast of his cannibalism, explaining that humans were saltier than leopards.

Some cognoscenti blame his behavior on advanced syphilis.

Vladimir Vladimirovich Putin (b. 1952)

Putin was *TIME* magazine's 2007 Person of the Year. You might be flummoxed to hear he was proposed for the 2014 Nobel Peace Prize in 2014.

He calls judo a "life philosophy."

Another of his tenets links homosexual marriage with Satanism.

Putin's social skills show a certain tone-deafness. He attended a ballet in 2013; while he may have enjoyed the production, however, he decided the intermission was the occasion for a grand public announcement of his divorce. In a meeting with Angela Merkel, he allowed his dog to harass her despite her evident fright.

Like many of your high-handed rulers, Putin lives high on the hog. Contents of his personal palace: a church, a theater, and a movie theater. Other all-season amenities: pool, ice palace, sauna, Turkish bath, casino, gas station, an eighty-seven-yard-long bridge, and an underground passage with a "tasting room." Putin is a developing story, so we'll pause here for the nonce. I'm sure you'll stay tuned.

Vladimir Lenin, founder, Russian Bolshevik Party (b. 1870)
Born Vladimir Ilyich Ulyanov, he restyled himself Lenin after the Siberian River Lena.

In the US, buildings are often renamed either to honor a major donor or to reflect political or cultural changes (e.g., Lincoln Center>Avery Fisher Hall>David Geffen Hall). Six University of Richmond buildings named after slavery-supporters have lost their names. Buildings at Harvard have been stripped of the name Sackler due to the family's unethical Oxycontin sales.

Out of politics and hubris, a whole city, Saint Petersburg, has also undergone a number of iterations of its name. The city was founded as *Sankt-Pieter-Burch* by Tsar Peter the Great. It was de-Westernized post-tsar into *Petrograd.* After Lenin's death Petrograd became Leningrad; in 1971, when religion became okay again, it cycled back to Sankt-Peterburg.

Lenin ended the free press, declaring that his personal government was unregulated by law.

After some cosmetic work to erase wrinkles and other flaws, Lenin's body is on display in his mausoleum in Red Square (no photos or talking, hands must remain in pockets, and men must wear hats). In 2016 the country allotted $224,000 for the preservation of his corpse; the Communist party forbids substituting a synthetic copy for his actual body.

Joseph Stalin, Ioseb Besarionis dze Jughashvili, Uncle Joe (b. 1878)
Like others before him, Stalin monkeyed with his own name: he discarded his Georgian baptismal name (above) for the more familiar *Stalin*—"Man of Steel."

Not content with a name change, the young Stalin also changed his birthday and age to help elude Tsarists. In 1925 he rebranded the city Tsaritsyn as Stalingrad (it was changed again in 1961 to Volgograd, "city on the Volga").

Stalin's father forced him into the family shoe factory at age twelve, his first and only job.

Although resourceful (he escaped incarceration in Siberia in a canoe), Stalin lacked physical charm. Smallpox had pitted his skin (blemishes that were photoshopped out in public pictures). His modest height earned him Truman's nickname, "The Little Squirt."

He ridiculed his guests, singling out for public mockery his minister Vyacheslav Molotov, better remembered for incendiary bombs—Molotov cocktails. Speaking of cocktails, Stalin also plied guests with drinks, hoping they'd rashly reveal secrets he could exploit.

Stalin upgraded *Zvezda,* the weekly party newspaper, into today's daily called *Pravda,* which means "Truth."

Like Putin, Stalin was nominated for the Nobel Peace Prize.

Adolf Hitler (b. 1889)
This entry is short, inversely proportional to Hitler's infamy. And his abominations are all too familiar.

Hitler claimed his father's best deed was changing the family name from Schicklgruber. We can understand this opinion: Schicklgruber means "moneygrubber," as in "shekel-grabber"—an association with Hebrew not to be tolerated.

Jung reported a pronounced femininity in Hitler's handwriting. Make of it what you will.

Hitler boasted of his vegetarianism, where his vegetarian diet (according to Albert Speer) included pork and other animal products.

Benito Amilcare Andrea Mussolini, Il Duce—compare Duke, above (b. 1883)

His Christian name means "blessed one," but his beliefs were whimsical. He believed certain individuals (for one, the King of Spain) could gaze at you with an evil eye and control your mind.

He invented fascism, which, despite his name, was no blessing. This philosophy took its name from the *fasces*, the ancient Roman symbol of authority; Mussolini liked the idea of ruling a neo-Roman Empire. Latin fasces were bundles of sticks with an axe blade sticking out of them. Wikipedia says the actual fasces *were a portable kit for flogging and decapitation.*

Reportedly, the fascist faction executed up to two thousand political enemies. Or sometimes, for a gentler purge, they dosed opponents with castor oil, causing runaway diarrhea.

To rectify Italy's economic slump, Mussolini urged Italians to hand over their jewels to his regime. In return they got a metal bracelet labelled with the catchy phrase "Gold for the Fatherland." What a deal.

Another of Il Duce's slogans, *Mussolini is Always Right,* proved you could completely trust him.

It's not astonishing that he was unpopular—during his life and beyond. Disguised in a German coat and helmet, he was caught and executed along with his girlfriend in Milan, where a mob shoved a rat into the dead dictator's mouth, shot him in the head, and urinated and spat on him.

His Excellency Generalissimo Francisco Franco (b. 1892)
He's said to have lost one of his testicles during a battle. This seems to be a thing with Spanish royalty. Three centuries earlier, we saw the same condition in Charles the Bewitched.

More significantly, Franco killed thirty thousand to fifty thousand subjects in the "social cleansing" of his White Terror. He took his "nationalism" seriously. He limited local languages, permitting only Basque, Catalan, and the Galician of his native region. Children had to be given strictly Spanish names.

To sync up with the Nazis, he put Spain on Central European Time, where it remains today—at variance even with Portugal.

Saddam Hussein (b.1937)
The name *Saddam* means "confronter." His atrocities are many and notorious, but here I'm concerned with the less familiar.

He wrote a romance novel (*Zabiba and the King*), which Amazon calls "an allegorical love story between a mighty king (Saddam) and a simple, yet beautiful commoner named Zabiba (the Iraqi people). Zabiba is married to a cruel and unloving husband (the United States) who forces himself upon her against her will. This act of rape is compared to the United States invasion of Iraq."

For Saddam, even *belles lettres* were political.

Biographer Saïd Aburish tended to exaggerate, but I do credit him when he reports Saddam's belief that he talked personally to God— who told him to make Iraq a leader of all Arab countries. God is handy to have available to take the rap.

Aiming to quash tribal solidarity, Saddam ordered his Ba'ath thugs to use their connections to track down his enemies, kill them, and kill their relatives too.

Saddam reportedly owned guns made of gold and a copy of the Qur'an written in blood (50 pints).

Osama bin Laden (b. 1957)

For Kim Jong-un, it was the Bulls and the Lakers. Bin Laden fancied the Arsenal Football Club. In his final hide-out in Abbottabad, he collected soccer and cricket balls lost by local kids: he repaid the young players, who began driving balls over the wall for the cash.

Bin Laden micro-managed—by which I mean repressed—his people. Western extravagances such as music and iced drinks were taboo. Like Kim Jong-un, however, Bin Laden was exempt from his own morality code—reminding us of Odysseus, who denied his sailors the experience of hearing the Sirens sing, but no problem for their captain, who was a higher-order human being.

The Wild West is the very essence of Western culture, and Bin Laden was so fond of Westerns that he even sported ten-gallon-hats. Luckily Kim Jong-un's tastes in Western lifestyle run to basketball. It's hard to picture him in a Stetson. At a pudgy five foot three inches and three hundred pounds, the North Korean dictator does not resemble the rangy Bin Laden—six foot six inches and 160 pounds.

Bin Laden also accumulated an impressive stash of pornography.

He underwrote his jihad work with his inheritance of almost $30 million. In Tora Bora he had a fancy (and fake) funeral in 2001—which did not hoodwink the world into believing he was dead. Pursuing him cost the United States (according to the *Atlantic Monthly*) over $3 trillion.

Nicolae Ceaușescu, Romanian President (b. 1918)

Unlike his compatriot Count Dracula, he's not a big household name, even if we could pronounce it. And keep track of who I'm talking about so I don't have to retype his name—bad enough to spell but the cedilla is the killer. Despite these inconveniences, a few items warrant consideration.

He wanted his wife Elena to be an asset, so he invented eminence for her as Romania's leading chemical researcher. So what if she was only marginally literate? Family biographer Edward Behr notes, she "didn't know what a chromatograph was and didn't recognize the formula for sulfuric acid." She pronounced CO_2 "co-two," earning her the Romanian nickname "Co-doi."

Ceaușescu required that the avenue to his "People's Palace" (second in size only to the Pentagon as biggest building in the world) would measure a meter wider than the Champs Élysées.

He designed what seems to be a drum majorette's baton and called it his "presidential sceptre." With respect to his public photographs, he stopped his age clock in his forties. Image mattered, even in an age before photoshop.

According to architect Alexandru Budistenu, "The sight of a church bothered Ceaușescu," who had them all razed or moved out of his personal ambit.

When a firing squad was about to kill him and his wife, Ceaușescu sang the Communist anthem, "The Internationale" (where the tune if not the text surpasses all other national anthems).

François Duvalier; Papa Doc, President of Haiti (b. 1907)
Duvalier gave himself the affectionate name to reflect his medical doctorate and his paternal-style care for his people. You decide about the fatherly part:

Duvalier founded the undercover paramilitary unit *Tonton Macoute*, named for a fictional monster who breakfasts on children. His own version of this outfit were not cannibals but garden-murderers who stoned Haitian citizens, burned them alive, and suspended the bodies from tree limbs as a deterrent to Duvalier's enemies.

You often get a big ego-display with dictators. Papa Doc fostered his own personality cult, in his case a personality *o*cult. The enslaved ancestors of many Haitians had brought Voodoo beliefs from West Africa. Papa Doc reinforced his power by posing as a Vodou avatar, but he covered his bases: He was "one with not only the *lwa* [spirits] but Jesus Christ and God himself": his public version of the Lord's Prayer replaces God with Duvalier. In a propaganda poster Jesus touches his shoulder saying He has chosen Papa Doc.

But that's not all, and here we move into derangement zone. Duvalier had some of the air above John F. Kennedy's tomb brought to him, to control JFK's soul. Soul-control was important: in order to talk with a certain rebel's soul (reports writer Karl Shaw), he kept an agitator's head in one of his cupboards. According to *TIME* magazine, Duvalier ordered the slaughter of all black dogs, claiming another of his opponents could turn himself into a black dog.

This was a man fond of watching prisoners placed in sulfuric acid.

Baby Doc (Papa's son); Jean-Claude Duvalier (b. 1951)
Baby Doc "governed" Haiti from 1971-1986. Torture and murder continued, resulting in mass emigration.

Taxpayers paid $2,000,000 for his 1980 wedding. Never mind that Haiti has the highest poverty rate in this hemisphere.

Fidel Castro (b. 1926)
Castro grew a beard, figuring that shaving wasted 5.5 thousand minutes annually; he thereby saved ten days a year.

It's reported that the CIA considered causing that iconic beard to fall out by covering his shoes with thallium. They also asked his ex-mistress to lace his cigars with the toxin botulin. Another rejected scheme was to lure the scuba-diving Castro with an explosive undersea seashell. Alternative: drop a fungal agent into his wetsuit or infect his scuba tank with TB. They proposed a pen concealing a deadly needle. Another thought involved spraying his radio studio with a hallucinogen to make nonsense of his speeches.

And if any of that is true, I feel a new respect for our Central Intelligence Agency.

Ernesto "Che" Guevara (b. 1928)
He was an MD whose specialty was leprosy before becoming the Castro regime's physician.

Cuba's Revolutionary Government outlawed a cologne created for Che: *Ernesto* was a presumably manly fragrance, a "woodsy and refreshing citric scent with notes of talcum powder." (See also J. Edgar Hoover below.)

The nickname "Che" means something like "Hey, pal."

His portrait titled "Guerrillero Heroico" has been called the most celebrated photograph of all time.

CRIMINALS AND PSYCHOPATHS

There's a very fine line, even imperceptible, between the people below and many of the dictators above who slaughtered millions. The only distinction is that the men below are not in politics.

I confess that this section is sensational. But, again, it's not that I revel in horrific and grotesque phenomena; but they come with the territory in a book focused on freakish.

John Wilkes Booth (b. 1838)

Booth's Plan A was to seize Lincoln as a hostage with the ransom demand that certain Confederate captives be freed. He killed the President due to his frustration when Lincoln didn't show up at the expected venue (a military hospital).

Jeffrey Dahmer (b. 1960)

Rapist, necrophiliac, cannibal, obsessive hoarder of body parts. In a thirteen-year period, spanning two states, this demented individual murdered seventeen people.

Animal bones had always fascinated Dahmer, who as a boy practiced dissection on roadkill. As a new high-school graduate, he murdered a hitchhiker he had hoped was, like himself, gay.

Dahmer, who was a proto-alcoholic in his teens, later lived with his grandmother. She finally kicked him out, partly because of the odors of decomposition in the cellar.

In his apartment, police eventually found human torsos, some skinned, in an industrial drum of acid and in the freezer; he had literal skeletons in the closet along with skulls, bleached or painted. Also, a pair of preserved penises. (He ate the organs, cooked with sauces and herbs to taste.)

He was saving these artifacts for an altar he was planning, *incorporating* (in the literal sense of the word) incense and blue lighting, with a leather chair nearby for convenient viewing.

In prison, he was later baptized in a whirlpool as a born-again Christian.

Jack the Ripper
To date, this individual is unidentified.

The "canonical five" are the subset of victims who were all killed within a few blocks in the fall of 1888.

Police were initially skeptical about a warning letter purportedly from the perpetrator: they believed it when its prediction of a cut ear on his next target was confirmed.

Charles Manson (b. 1934)
His birth certificate identified him as "No Name Maddox." Ms. Maddox, his mother, later sold him in exchange for a pint of ale. (He was retrieved by her brother.)

Manson's fiancée reported that he was willing to wed her only if she in turn promised to exhibit him in a glass coffin after his death, possibly channeling Snow White.

Prison inmates often adopt religion. Unlike Dahmer, Manson went Scientologist.

Lorena Bobbitt (b. 1969)

Who is this person and why would I include her here? Well, she's a unique individual and I have nowhere else to put her. And if she isn't a household word, she deserves to be.

Her sole but spectacular claim to fame is that, in 1993, Lorena Bobbitt bobbed not her hair but her abusive fiancé's penis, saying he had raped her. She threw his severed member out of her car window, eventually stopping to alert 911 of the organ's approximate location, which allowed it to be reunited with his body. The complicated surgery required nine hours.

Like the Bobbit worm, a benthic bristle-worm that is "a sexually reproducing organism *that lacks external reproductive organs,*" John Wayne Bobbitt lost his (see Gadaleta, M. V. *et. al,* 2008). But a man named John Wayne needs his manhood. *John Wayne Bobbitt* started a (failed) rock band: "The Severed Parts." Staying with the entertainment industry, he played the lead role in porn movies such as John Wayne Bobbitt's *Frankenpenis.*

Later, after two weeks served in jail for domestic battery, he became a Universal Life Church minister, specializing in marriages. Yet another prisoner gone pious.

As for Lorena, she was sentenced to six weeks in a mental hospital and went on to start Lorena's Red Wagon, a group to combat spousal abuse.

QUACKS AND
CHEATERS

The provenance of the term *quack* is Dutch *kwakzalver*—a raucously blathering hawker of salve (although only one of the four quacks below actually sells ointment). The classic unguent quack, for example, is the self-styled Rattlesnake King, Clark Stanley, original *snake oil* purveyor of a Hopi tribal medicine.

The impotence sector is another perennial growth industry; impotence "cures" are always a good come-on. (Products like William J. Bailey's *RadiThor*—radium-laced water—may have helped also cure longevity.) A rival of Bailey's inserted a goat scrotum into men's genitalia—or, for $5,000, used human testicles from men awaiting capital punishment: this was John Brinkley, forward thinker in the field of xenotransplanation.

But I cite those just to introduce one familiar quack and his eponymous pseudo-science.

Franz Mesmer (b. 1734)
The German doctor Franz Mesmer said his personal form of hypnosis could elicit from the human body a substance from outer space which he called *animal magnetism* (*Lebensmagnetismus*). Here's a mini-mesmerism manual:

Method 1 (private patient). Stroke your subject's arms before moving on to his or her *hypochondrium* under the rib cage. Frequently Mesmer's patients, call them credulous if you like, felt weird internal motions under his hands. Mesmer would simultaneously stroke a glass harmonica if it fit the occasion. Speaking of fitting, some of his subjects went into fits—*crises* in Mesmer's jargon—which preceded healing. This therapy released harmful forces in the bodily humors. You can also call these crises *titillations délicieuses*, as he did, and from which you may conclude that 1) he was good at selling his clients a bill of goods, and/or 2) these private sessions provided services beyond cures.

In 1790, one John Pearson revealed some anonymous letters describing Method 1 results, with vomiting at the "crisis." At this point your subject is in a "remarkable state" (I'd use a less polite word than "remarkable") where items grow "luminous and transparent" and where he can even see inside himself to the cause of his sickness. I'd throw up too if I had to inspect my own viscera.

Method 2 (group entertainment). Place on the floor a vat (with holes in its cover) huge enough for a score of suckers to gather around it. In one hole tie a wire to a protruding magnetized iron rod and hand it to one participant who'll act as a conduit. The folks hold hands and hook up with "nature's forces."

Benjamin Franklin, who accused Mesmer of quackery, helped hasten his downfall. Mesmer was discredited and denied the right to practice medicine.

Let's move on to three athlete-quacks.

Rosie Ruiz (b. 1953)
This woman's hoaxes were executed with every conceivable dim-witted mistake. So embarrassing. Example: During the course of one marathon, she was seen on the subway taking a shortcut to the finish line. Ruiz was also witnessed breaking through the spectators onto the course half a mile before the race's terminus. She could

not remember course details that all the runners knew. The actual woman winner, who was ahead at the eighteenth mile, hadn't seen Ruiz overtake her. None of the photos or videos showed her during the race. Although her body was not noticeably fit, she wasn't sweating when she finished the 26.2 miles and even with her automotive assist, her heart rate was too elevated for a true marathoner. (She explained that she woke up that day "with a lot of energy.")

In the 1980 Boston Marathon, Ruiz was the first woman to cross the finish line—the fastest women's time ever recorded in the race and among the top three women in the history of marathons. In fact, she'd impressively shaved twenty-five minutes off her marathon time of six months earlier.

Ruiz applied late for the New York Marathon, but because she said she had terminal brain cancer, the committee made an exception for her.

Lance Armstrong (b. 1971)
If Rosie Ruiz was a witless amateur, cyclist Armstrong was a pro. The United States Anti-Doping Agency called Armstrong's cheating "the most sophisticated, professionalized and successful doping program that sport has ever seen."

Armstrong had a sense of humor, though. Alluding to his cancer of the testicle, the *Huffington Post* reported that Armstrong named a café he owns the "Juan Pelota Café," where *pelota* = "ball."

Tonya Harding (b. 1970)
Just before the 1994 figure-skating competition, Tonya Harding plotted to keep her rival Nancy Kerrigan *hors de combat* by hiring two hitmen. Injuring Kerrigan's leg, they accomplished their mission.

Piltdown Man
Piltdown Man is not a person. He's famous for *not* being a person. He's a skull and jawbone unearthed in an English town in 1907. The bones were a potpourri of human and ape pieces smoothed and stained to resemble an early human, a fossil that hoaxer Charles Dawson touted as the elusive missing link between men and other primates. (Not to be confused with Charles Darwin, who temporarily plummeted in my esteem as either fool or fellow fraudster at first glance.)

In 1949, scientists showed the Piltdown bones to date back a mere fifty thousand years—a time when *homo sapiens* had already been around for a while.

Annie Dookhan, née Annie Sadiyya Khan (b. 1977)
I'll finish with a name only marginally familiar, even in Boston where she pulled her stunts.

Dookhan, a chemist in a Massachusetts state laboratory, lied about having a master's degree and being enrolled in Harvard PhD courses. Meanwhile she was entering fake lab-test results, occasionally mixing the samples with cocaine. I can see faking the tests out of sloppiness, say, or even out of haste, but the cocaine was a gratuitous, not to say malicious, touch.

Her prosecutor alleged her deceit cost the state "millions and millions" of dollars in untangling the disaster and its effect on patients' health. The governor revoked the lab's license. Her sentence (2013) was three to five years in prison.

AMERICAN GOVERNMENT FIGURES

Benjamin Franklin (b. 1706)

Franklin was a flirt. French ladies loved his backwoodsy fur hat, which I would describe as ridiculous—unlike the coonskin cap later worn with such charm by Davy Crockett. Franklin's version lacked the ringed raccoon-tail.

In the vanguard about health—as about many things, Franklin took "air baths" seated naked at the window.

Inventions:

- Edible scent to perfume the odor of farts.
- Bifocal lenses and daylight savings.
- A *glass armonica*: thirty-seven glass bowls, their colors indicating the notes. Franz Mesmer hypnotized clients by undulating his hands in time with the armonica's spooky background tones. The public believed its sound would provoke seizures and insanity, but it was good enough for the likes of Beethoven and Richard Strauss to use it in their compositions.
- A bladder catheter (for his brother).
- The volunteer fire department.
- The expression that the only perennial things are death and taxes.

Franklin encouraged men to pick oldish mistresses, and to "shun bimbos," for the reasons that they provided support in your old age, built-in birth control, and had less disease than in mostly younger prostitutes. He concluded that, in bed at night, you can't see them anyway.

When Franklin died, France held a national day of mourning. Very posthumous: in 1999, Franklin was inducted into the Chess Hall of Fame.

Alexander Hamilton (b. 1757)

Because he was illegitimate, it was illegal for him to go to school.

If he aspired to become president, he shouldn't have aired his seamy relations with someone else's wife.

To defend his honor after Hamilton had publicly slighted him, Aaron Burr challenged him to a duel. Hamilton accepted, reluctantly. The opponents executed the customary paces and shot: Hamilton lost, lethally.

The rest is history and as such of no interest to us.

Lafayette; Marquis Marie-Joseph-Paul-Yves-Roch-Gilbert du Motier de La Fayette (b. 1757)

Not American, but close enough.

Ancestors, legendary: One forebear discovered Christ's Crown of Thorns. Another was Joan of Arc's fellow-soldier.

Raised in a fancy French castle, he quipped, "It's not my fault." His comment on his name: "I was baptized like a Spaniard, with the name of every conceivable saint who might offer me more protection in battle."

The only battles he fought were in America. In fact, his tomb in France is covered in soil brought from Bunker Hill.

J. Edgar Hoover, Hypocrite Supreme (b. 1895)

Rumors circulated that he had a sexual relationship with FBI colleague Clyde Tolson. They commuted, lunched, and vacationed together and occasionally came to the office in matching clothes. Tolson was Hoover's principal heir.

Then there was the Lavender Scare, when Hoover (possibly hypocritically) had President Eisenhower fire federal employees reckoned homosexual. Hoover also sacked female employees when he took his FBI job. He himself wore ladies' perfume.

Reports allege Hoover denied the existence of the Mafia because it was blackmailing him about his homosexuality.

He went to the races when the nation was mourning Martin Luther King Jr. Oddly, another rumor—based on youthful photos—whispered that he had Black forebears.

His porn library was possibly even bigger than Bin Laden's.

King George knighted Hoover for doing a few pieces of espionage work for Britain.

Eleanor Roosevelt (b. 1884)

Though not a political *official*, she was another Washington personage beset by rumors of homosexuality—which marginally gives me the occasion to slip her in. Besides, she's too formidable a person to list under the book's Presidents section as mere adjunct to her husband.

Her height of five feet ten inches helped make her a strong athlete. She claimed that the best event in her whole life was selection to her school's first team in field hockey, a debatable "best" for a woman with a resume like hers. What she loathed was her year as a debutante, and no objection from me on that one.

Amelia Earhart took Eleanor flying, inspiring her to take pilot's lessons.

The AP reporter covering Eleanor Roosevelt, Lorena Hickok, eventually left her job: Lorena was a lesbian and concerned about her lack of perspective when writing about a woman who fascinated her personally. Letters that they exchanged indicate a physical relationship. The two women went to the theater or had dinner *à deux* at Hickok's place almost daily. Lorena gave her a sapphire ring, and Eleanor wrote up to fifteen notes per day to her, telling her that she kissed her picture twice a day.

History esteems Eleanor Roosevelt for her work in multiple fields. If I've offered these trivia and omitted her many positive influences on American life, it's as usual because celebrated accomplishments aren't in my purview.

US PRESIDENTS

John Adams (b. 1735)

He suggested President Washington be called "His Majesty" and/or "His Highness."

Adams himself was ridiculed with the title "His Rotundity."

He and Thomas Jefferson both died on July 4, 1826, when the Declaration of Independence was exactly fifty years old.

John Quincy Adams (b. 1767)

Enjoyed skinny-dipping in the Potomac.

The Marquis de Lafayette gave him an alligator which he kept in the bathroom.

Chester A. Arthur (b. 1829)

We have talked about royal heads of state and their crowns. If Chester A. Arthur had worn a crown, it would have been a bag over his head.

What can we say of him? His parents named him after the obstetrician who delivered him: Chester Abell, a dorky name that aligns with his nonentity. I researched boys' names for examples of any especially unusual/memorable ones that might have boosted his brand. My hypothesis fell flat when I ran across this, which I'm not making up:

What is the rarest boys' name?

The rarest baby boy name is Rome, but other rare baby boy names include Chester, Henley, and Maynard.

He sold the White House furniture to be able to afford new décor, for which he hired top-dollar Louis Comfort Tiffany, who, unlike Chester A. Arthur, *is* a household name. Arthur valued personal adornment, too; he was known as "The Dude President."

Well, I've done my best in four paragraphs. He must now sink back into oblivion.

James Buchanan (b. 1791)

He was accident-prone. Here's a doubly humiliating misadventure: When his buttocks underwent an archery mishap, he had to hand over his spot on the Lewis and Clark Expedition—to a woman: Sacagawea.

The name of James's childhood pet African Gray Parrot was Betsy Ross, suggesting the patriotic role for which he was destined. At the White House he kept a herd of pygmy goats.

Buchanan was the only president who never married. Buchanan's bachelor status and his close friendship with Senator William Rufus King (Alabama), with whom he lived, triggered gossip. Andrew Jackson nicknamed the pair "Miss Nancy and Aunt Fancy." When the Senator left Washington for another job, Buchanan complained: "I am now solitary and alone, having no companion in the house with me. I have gone a-wooing several gentlemen but have not succeeded with any one of them."

Because he was ambivalent about abolition, another nickname was "Doughface," which the dictionary defines as a Northern congressman not opposed to slavery in the South. It was during his presidency that the outcome of the *Dred Scott* case denied citizenship to African Americans.

George W. ("Dubya") *Bush* (b. 1946)

Not an A student. Bush Jr. attended the academically elite Phillips Andover school. About teachers' corrections on his exams, he said "the impression of the red marker was so intense that it stuck out of the back side of the blue book."

The English language was to him *terra incognita*. Handcuffs became "cufflinks." Enthralling became "inebriating." Once he got a zero for a pitiful gaffe: consulting a thesaurus, he avoided repeating the word "tears" (as in weeping) by describing the "lacerates" running down someone's cheeks. Possibly he ignored his own precept that "reading is the basics [sic] for all learning."

But no more quotations, lest I fall into the trap he accused others of: "They misunderestimated me."

George H. W. Bush (b. 1924)
"I'm President of the United States, and I'm not going to eat any more broccoli!"

Jimmy Carter (b. 1924)
After observing an unidentifiable thing in the sky, he claimed he'd now unseal all UFO files. For security reasons, he then had second thoughts.

Grover Cleveland (b. 1837)
Not in any way to belittle Cleveland's stature, but the better-known Grover is a character on Sesame Street.

This president's main claim to fame (I claim) was an event he concealed: Diagnosed with oral cancer, he had a piece of his jaw replaced by rubber. To prevent public panic, the operation was done secretly on a friend's yacht. And this skullduggery meant leaving his mustache intact, which made for tricky surgery.

If you don't believe me about the rubber, maybe you'll believe the National Institutes of Health report which also clarifies the procedure for the layperson:

"President Grover Cleveland had a clandestine resection of a maxillary tumor in July, 1893. The resection left the president with a large defect in his palate. . . . a rubber obturator perfectly reconstructed Cleveland's face and allowed for normal speech."

Bill Clinton; Clinton William Jefferson Blythe III (b. 1946)
Clinton eats the seeds and the core of apples. I have no data on the stem.

The teenage Clinton memorized the whole "I Have a Dream" address right after Martin Luther King Jr. gave it.

But most of his career is too familiar to belong here.

Calvin Coolidge (b. 1872)
Coolidge was *born* on the Fourth of July (whereas Jefferson, Adams, and Munroe had *died* on that date).

Coolidge was given a Liberian pygmy hippo, William "Billy" Johnson Hippopotamus. Billy mostly lived at the zoo, but for company Coolidge also had a pet raccoon who raced around the residence and wrecked the furnishings.

When security concerns forbade horseback riding, Coolidge rigged up an electric saddle that trotted and cantered. He put it through its paces thrice daily for exercise. I doubt Peloton offers a product with equine gaits.

During breakfast, a servant routinely rubbed Coolidge's head with Vaseline. He believed petroleum jelly promoted good health, although the German consumer-organization *Stiftung Warentest* detected excessive hydrocarbons in this "Wonder Jelly."

In a tennis game, his sixteen-year-old son suffered a blister which became fatally septic and killed him, a tragic story often repeated by my mother as a cautionary tale.

Dwight D. Eisenhower; "Ike" (b. 1890)
He renamed the official presidential getaway-spot after his grandson: "Camp David." FDR had styled it Shangri-la, which I call a vile name and Ike called "just a little too fancy for a Kansas farm boy." The real name of the retreat, of course, is *Naval Support Facility Thurmont*, originally *Hi-Catoctin*, family housing for federal employees.

Ike took his golf seriously; in 2000 he was named *Golfweek's* Golfer of the Century.

Millard Fillmore (b. 1800)
He first entered politics on an anti-Freemasonry platform.

An unnamed history professor at Yale (writing for an *American Heritage* article) opined: "Even to discuss Chester Arthur or Millard Fillmore is to overrate them."

James Garfield (b. 1831)
As an ambidextrous classicist, Garfield was able to write simultaneously in Greek with one hand and in Latin with the other.

After a month and a half in the White House, Garfield was shot by an unsuccessful candidate for a post in the French embassy. His death was not a good one. Garfield lost eighty pounds. It was 1881, and since IV feeding tubes were currently unavailable, the doctors gave him nutrient enemas. I wonder how those worked.

He lay on his bed in his New Jersey summer house, where a crude metal detector seeking the bullet located only the bedsprings, whereupon his physicians rummaged around inside his body, causing the infection that killed him. You can see his bullet-pierced spine today at the National Museum of Health and Medicine.

Gerald Ford, born *Leslie Lynch King Jr.* (b. 1913)
He took his stepfather's name.

His wife's social and political impact is too familiar to belong here, but I'll touch on it anyway. First Lady Betty Ford, *TIME* magazine's 1975 "Woman of the Year," was a gift to women. With the publicly-shared story of her radical mastectomy, she considerably raised awareness about breast cancer. Another significant contribution was her openness about her treatment for alcoholism and chemical dependency. She also championed the Equal Rights Amendment.

Ulysses S. Grant (b. 1822)
He came by the initial S through a clerical error in his application to West Point. "US," however, were handy initials to have in his line of work.

He commanded the Union Army, an even more admirable feat when we learn he was afraid of the sight of blood.

Warren Harding (b. 1865)
I'll limit my comments to his Airedale, Laddie Boy, who was fêted at lavish birthdays, granted newspaper interviews, and honored by a statue in the Smithsonian Institute.

Laddie Boy had a special seat at cabinet meetings, which he attended wearing a collar fabricated with Gold Rush nuggets.

Benjamin Harrison; "The Human Iceberg" (b. 1833)
Unfamiliar with electricity, Harrison was terrified of electrocution. He would leave the White House lights on rather than use the redoubtable lamp switch.

By the Land Revision Act, Harrison initiated the system of National Parks and Nature Reserves, starting with Yellowstone.

Bad beards have appeared in these pages and will appear again. Harrison was the last bearded president. His beard's facial footprint is acceptable, but I take exception to a beard ending in a repulsive frill of curls.

William Henry Harrison; "Kid Glove Harrison"; "Old Tippecanoe" (b. 1773)

Because of his sensitive skin, he wore kid gloves, an accessory that didn't necessarily go over well on the rough-and-tumble political scene.

He died a month into his presidency. Everyone knows that standing in icy rain during your long inauguration speech does *not* give you a cold (which is a virus), but people cited a chill as his cause of death.

Some claimed he succumbed to influenza despite best-practice protocols of opium and enema. Others posit that the sewage deposits near the White House gave him fatal gastro enteritis. Wiser people knew he died of *Tecumseh's Curse*, which predicted that any president elected in a year ending in zero would die in office.

Harrison did know the Shawnee chief Tecumseh—or at least he had challenged Tecumseh's brother, a *soi-disant* sorcerer, to "cause the sun to stand still, the moon to alter its course, the rivers to cease to flow or the dead to rise from their graves." Like Twain's time-travelling Connecticut Yankee, the Shawnee seer used an eclipse of the sun as a demo to lend the curse some credibility.

Rutherford B. Hayes; "Granny Hayes"; "The Great Unknown"; *"Rutherfraud"; his "Fraudulency"* (b. 1822)

His last two nicknames arose from his disputed presidential election, a still-familiar circumstance. He won by one vote.

Hayes's White House was dry. His teetotaler wife was "Lemonade Lucy." No dancing, no smoking, no card games. These abstemious habits earned him the label "Granny Hayes."

Hayes owned the first Siamese cat in America.

When Alexander Graham Bell installed the first phone ever in the White House, President Hayes's phone number was "1."

Herbert Hoover (b. 1874)

A Quaker.

Sometimes the Hoovers spoke Mandarin to foil would-be listeners.

Hoover's son had two pet alligators. Where J. Q. Adams had kept his in the East Room, the Hoover reptiles crawled around the gardens.

Roosevelt rejected the name Hoover Dam and christened it the Boulder Dam. Only later was the original name reestablished.

Andrew Jackson (b. 1767)

His *New York Times* obituary dubbed Jackson "the most unpopular public man that had ever held any office in the United States." So much for *nil nisi bonum*. Nor did flags fly at half-mast.

Jackson had crippling stage fright, inconvenient for a US president.

Every time someone disparaged his wife, Jackson challenged the person to a duel. Close to a hundred times. (But compare this to Frederick Barbarossa's mule-genitalia sentence for a similar offense.)

Someone gave him a cheddar cheese weighing 1.5 tons. It remained in the lobby of the White House for twenty-four months.

His parrot Poll shouted shocking profanities at his burial.

Thomas Jefferson (b. 1743)

He invented the swivel chair.

We have Jefferson to thank for the first ice cream recipe: six egg yolks, a half-pound of sugar, two bottles of cream, and one vanilla bean. Less appealing to guests were the tomatoes Jefferson grew. People watched in horror while he ate one of these mysterious and disgusting items.

Another feature of his garden was the opium poppy *Papaver somniferum*. The DEA got wind of the plants in 1991 and ordered their eradication from Monticello.

His pet mockingbird Dick flew around his office, frequently singing along with the president's violin.

You yourself can visit his octagonal house, Poplar Forest, built to his exact specifications, where he employed over ninety slaves to look after it. He loved octagons (eight-sided spaces maximized interior light). And the gift shop: if the house privy on a refrigerator magnet doesn't appeal, consider a Jefferson finger-puppet.

Andrew Johnson (b. 1808)
Apprenticed, by which I mean quasi-enslaved, to a tailor as a boy, he sometimes made his own clothing as President.

He was the first president to be impeached (for firing his Secretary of War).

Lyndon Baines Johnson (b. 1908)
According to his biographer Robert Caro, Johnson met with his staff members while on the toilet. He called his own member "Jumbo," and he took great pride in its size.

John F. Kennedy (b. 1917)
On three occasions he came so close to dying that the Last Rites were performed.

JFK was a speed-reader. You and I average 250 to 300 words per minute; his rate was supposedly 1200. He must have aced the brutal reading-comprehension sections on standardized tests.

James Madison (b. 1751)

Madison loved ice cream, which he stored in his two-story icehouse. Americans' preferred flavors at the time were asparagus, Parmesan, and chestnut, but his wife Dolley's favorite was oyster.

Madison was on the tiny side. At five foot four inches tall he weighed a hundred pounds, a figure I can't personally believe. But he may have had a weak stomach; he originally considered the Bill of Rights a "nauseous project."

Madison had trouble projecting his voice, which made his public speaking quasi-inaudible. After he had declined a doctor's offer to stave off his death until July 4, his dying words: "I always talk better lying down."

For *The Guinness Book of World Records*, if the fact were verifiable: One woman deemed him "the most unsociable creature in existence."

James Madison and Thomas Jefferson were arrested for taking a carriage ride on a Sunday.

He claimed he would have won the 1777 election if he had plied the electorate with free alcohol.

William McKinley (b. 1843)

Greeting the audience at an exposition, McKinley gave his good-luck carnation to a twelve-year-old named Myrtle. This turned out to be a bad move. A minute later he was shot. After seeming to recover, he complained of pain; but the laxatives he was given (purges being the perennial panacea) failed to arrest the fatal gangrene coursing through his body.

In 1901 he declined a doctor's offer to keep him from dying until July 4.

James Monroe; "The Last of the Cocked Hats" (b. 1758)

Monroe was luckier in his demise. Like Jefferson and Adams, he died on the Fourth of July.

Liberia's capital Monrovia—where freed slaves could settle—is named in his honor.

Richard Nixon; "Tricky Dick" (b. 1913)
Nixon was raised in a seriously Quaker family; they attended meetings four times on the Sabbath; he graduated from the Quaker college Whittier.

In the White House, Ike's personal recreation facility was a backyard golf green; Nixon had his own bowling alley in the basement.

Nixon exited the White House in disgrace, but we can credit his administration for founding the Environmental Protection Agency, broadening the Voting Rights Act, and establishing Title IX.

Barack Obama (b. 1961)
Again, this president's public life is well known—some of his private life, too, thanks to Michelle Obama's biography *Becoming*. Only two minutiae:

In high school, he used to be called "O'Bomber" for his basketball skills.

While studying at Harvard, he applied to be featured in a Black pin-up calendar.

Franklin Pierce, "Fainting Frank"; "Hero of Many a Well-Fought Bottle" (b. 1804)
Alcoholic.

When he didn't win the nomination for a second term, "There's nothing left to do but get drunk."

James Polk; "The Dark Horse Candidate" (b. 1795)
Outstandingly boring.

Unlike Franklin Pierce, Polk was no dipso: Sam Houston deplored his "use of water as a beverage." His wife Sarah forbade liquor—and dancing too for good measure.

Supposedly and unaccountably (and unlike Polk himself), Sarah was very popular. And she was attractive. The mid-century ringlets did her no favors, in my opinion, but you can't fault her for following fashion.

Polk held "office hours" open to any citizen who wanted to drop in. (He was mostly besieged by job applicants).

Ronald Reagan (b. 1911)

Some US presidents were (dubiously) qualified for the job by military know-how. In Reagan's case it was his Hollywood experience that equipped him for gubernatorial and presidential office. But holding the world's top job did not free him from bitterness over the lack of an Oscar.

He earned profound respect for his measured decisions made in consultation with an astrologer.

During the Red Scare, Reagan (agent "T-10") gave the FBI intel about actors who were possible Communists or other fellow travelers. Artists of any sort, of course, are always prone to sedition, if not outright treason.

Reagan used jellybeans to wean himself off pipe smoking. And I'm solidly with him in liking licorice best.

On the other hand, I can't say our literary tastes jibe. His favorite book was the Bible.

A gun fired close to Reagan on a movie set left him partly deaf.

Franklin Roosevelt (b. 1882)

When he declared war on Japan, Roosevelt decided the nation's wartime austerity effort had limits: "I honestly feel that it would be best for the country to keep baseball going."

Roosevelt probably contracted polio at a Boy Scout camp. In any case, garden golf or basement bowling were not for him. He replaced the White House cloakroom with a movie theater.

As an abundance of caution, FDR ordered Japanese Americans to be interned even before the countries were at war. As we know, he practiced that same xenophobia throughout the war. Note: avoid the cliché "abundance of caution."

Roosevelt's terrier was named "Murray the Outlaw of Fala Hill."

It was FDR who said: "The only thing we have to fear, is fear itself."

Theodore Roosevelt; "Rough Rider"; "Bwana Tumbo"; "Mr. Unusually Large Belly" (b. 1858)

Not a close relation to FDR.

Child taxidermist (not *of* children but *as* a child).

Speaking of stuffed objects: After he rescued a baby bear, teddy bears came onto the scene. Too bad he disliked the name "Teddy."

T. R. hosted a permanent menagerie at the White House, including reptiles, bears, a lion, a zebra, and an "affectionate" rat.

Toting food supplies and *Anna Karenina*, he once hunted down a gang of boat thieves, who would surely have outrun him had he been reading the weightier *War and Peace*.

Roosevelt was a prophetic environmentalist: "What will happen when our forests are gone, when the coal, the iron, the oil and the gas are exhausted, when the soils have been still further impoverished and washed into the streams, polluting the rivers, denuding the fields . . ." He created five national parks.

Appalled by the number of football injuries, Roosevelt convened Ivy League managers about increasing the game's safety. This effort would end in the Mr. Clean costumes players wear today.

He did not want to "cheapen" the motto "In God We Trust" by inscribing it on coins.

For all Roosevelt's religious sensibilities, he (according to Henry Adams) "showed the singular primitive quality that belongs to ultimate matter—the quality that medieval theology assigned to God—he was pure act."

William Taft; "Big Lub"; "Big Bill" (b. 1857)

He was what the airlines call a person of size. He did slim down from over 350 pounds to 260. Fat but incisively perceptive, he observed "too much flesh is bad for any man," a nice piece of iambic pentameter verse. It took six men to haul him out of the custom-built bathtub where he'd become wedged, making him a literal tub of lard. Its capacity was four persons (or 340 pounds).

Qualification: Possibly this event is a rumor-based bathtub overflow (Archimedes' displacement rule.) We'll renew our acquaintance with Archimedes when we investigate scientists.

At the White House, his personal cow (name: Pauline Wayne) gave him reliably fresh milk. Subsequently, however, as the first president to own a car, he changed the stable into a garage.

But he didn't like being President, and he quit after one term—whereas many fourth-year presidents grip the White House like a limpet.

Zachary Taylor; "Old Rough-and-Ready" (b. 1784)

Taylor's battle dress—ragged farming garb—earned him his nickname.

He died from contaminated cherries, unless it was the raw milk he drank with them. Before pasteurization, you had your pick of infections. Salmonella, E. coli, Campylobacter, Staphylococcus aureus, Yersinia, Brucella, and Listeria. Or maybe it was the cure that killed him: calomel, which is a mercury mixture.

Harry S. Truman (b. 1884)
His name: The *S* was an empty initial inserted by his parents in honor of a few family surnames. Since it wasn't an abbreviation, Truman omitted a period after the *S*. *The Chicago Manual of Style* told him, and still tells us, that a period here is mandatory. To avoid the drudgery of writing a period, to say nothing of the time wasted in lifting his pen to leave a space between his names, he signed himself HarrySTruman.

Before we dismiss this nanosecond time-saving notion as nonsense, let's recall that some of the sharpest minds would see his point. Recall Castro computing that shaving wasted 5.5 thousand minutes annually.

Apropos of Cuba, Truman was the first to describe Communism creep with the term *domino theory*.

Stay with me here: Another of Truman's game-related idioms was "passing the buck." The expression began as poker jargon (passing the next dealer a buck knife). Truman varied the phrase in a sign on his desk, "The buck stops here."

Even as Roosevelt's vice president, he wasn't informed that the US had an atomic bomb until the day he became President.

Donald Trump (b. 1946)
Words fail.

Martin Van Buren; "Old Kinderhook"; "Martin Van Ruin" (b. 1782)
The latter nickname reflects the stock market crash during his presidency.

He may be the most-often-commemorated president ever: his resounding legacy is (allegedly) the word *okay*. He was born in the town of Kinderhook and sometimes called "Old Kinderhook." His campaign slogan was "OK!" (Another origin proposed is a misspelling "oll korrekt" for "all correct," but let's pick the Van Buren hypothesis if only because this entry is about Van Buren and not about silly spelling.)

He was the first US president actually born in America. But he was raised speaking Dutch as his mother tongue and only learned English at school.

He founded the anti-slavery Free Soil Party.

George Washington (b. 1732)
If you've been believing Washington's dentures were made of wood, you've been believing wrong. They were made of bone, hippopotamus ivory, animal and human teeth, lead, brass screws and gold wire. If these materials sound dodgy, consider the Etruscans (circa sixth-century BC). They attached your teeth to animal ones with gold wire.

As mentioned above, with a book on famous people you get a fair amount of Father of this and Father of that. But George Washington was something special in the fatherhood field. The *Founder of the Day* site says: "George Washington was more than just the Father of His Country, he was also the Father of the American Mule." Our first president was also our first importer and breeder of mules.

Speaking of horses, let's clarify a few details about Washington's death. After a snowy day out riding and eating supper in damp clothes, he woke to a sore throat caused *again, not* by exposure to cold weather, but to a *germ*. I've mentioned that President Harrison's death was explained by this medical myth.

Washington died of quinsy, a quaint term for beta-hemolytic streptococcus, more familiar to us as fulminant acute epiglottitis, suppuration of tonsillar tissue or remaining tissue at the upper tonsillar pole.

Any doctor will tell you, "Aspiration of the abscess is the gold standard in management." Washington did not receive gold-standard treatment, which wasn't available until the 1900 Gold Standard Act.

What he did get was the usual enema; dried beetles applied to his throat; and a gargle of vinegar, molasses, and butter, better for a marinade than for abscess management. They also drained him of 40 percent of his blood.

Washington suffered from taphophobia: he lived in mortal terror of being buried alive. He ordered his burial delayed for three days post-mortem. The doctors waited and duly ascertained his death, unless the Father of our Country lives among us as a zombie.

Woodrow Wilson (b. 1856)
Wilson vetoed the Prohibition Act because it would operate during a war (the veto was overridden that same day).

He entered World War I to (famously) "make the world safe for democracy."

Equally vital, he arranged for movie equipment for solders so they could watch Charlie Chaplin.

In 1919, Wilson won the Nobel Peace Prize for founding the League of Nations. (Stalin, Putin, and Hitler were only nominated.)

BRITISH POLITICAL LEADERS

Winston Churchill, KG, OM, CH, TD, DL, FRS, RA (b. 1874)
Another accident-prone individual: Kidney rupture after a fall from
a bridge. Near-drowning in Switzerland. Dislocation of his shoulder
on a gangway in India. Plane crash during a flying lesson. Close call
with a car on Fifth Avenue.

Churchill understood the value of various venial vices:

During Prohibition in America, he wangled a medical order to
permit him an "indefinite" quantity of alcohol. Perhaps drinking
helped treat his "Black Dog"—a tendency to depression. A Churchill
Martini was pure gin—the only unmixed cocktail that exists. His
recipe: "I would like to observe the vermouth from across the room
while I drink my martini."

Churchill's "life pod" on a plane was a pressure chamber containing
an ashtray and air-purifying device.

A rumor says he ended his rousing "We shall fight on the beaches"
speech with a *sotto voce,* "And we'll fight them with the butt ends of
broken beer bottles because that's bloody well all we've got!"

Words on his grave: "I am ready to meet my Maker. Whether
my Maker is prepared for the great ordeal of meeting me is
another matter."

Margaret Thatcher, LG, OM, DStJ, PC, FRS (b. 1925)
As a commercial chemist, she worked to add air to ice cream,
resulting in the *Mr Whippy* brand.

Unfortunately fictional, Margaret Thatcher was portrayed as the rival of Lord Buckethead, a candidate backed by the Official Monster Raving Loony Party in the *Star Wars* parody film *Hyperspace* (2017). His platform included replacement of the city of Birmingham with a space station; elimination of the House of Lords (himself excepted); allocation of 100 billion pounds for Trident missiles—as you know, submarine-launched ballistic missiles (SLBM) equipped with multiple independently targetable reentry vehicles (MIRV). He defends these the cost of these weapons on the grounds that "no one will ever know" about a craft hidden underwater.

Lord Antony Lambton, Tory MP (b. 1922)
Lambton represented the town of Chester-le-Street, named for a paved Roman road.

This man entertained me at the Villa Cetinale, a seventeenth-century palace where he "retired" with his mistress after a brief career as junior defense minister. Sex and drug scandals made his resignation inevitable. A newspaper photo showed him in a compromising position with two women, one of them a dope-smoking dominatrix. He said he needed these pursuits because his government work was a waste of time. A friend of mine told me Lord Lambton had tried to push his wife, Bindy, into the fireplace.

Two facts about Lambton's villa salon, the only room I visited: On the wall hung old paintings; Lambton was interested only in their elaborate frames, which he collected. In this room a guest looked in vain for a place to sit. There were two sofas in front of the fireplace, but these seemed to be reserved for several sizable dogs. During meals these dogs were fed on food tossed from the table.

MILITARY

Julius Caesar (b. 100 BCE)
Birth: the obstetrical term *caesarean* does not derive from Caesar's birth but from the verb *caedere*, "to cut."
 Death: You can now visit the probably-apocryphal site of his assassination.

Oliver Hazard Perry; "Hero of Lake Erie" (b. 1785)
He originated the sentence "Don't Give Up the Ship."
 Perry fought the French in something called the *Quasi War* at the end of the eighteenth century. This mini campaign was sanctioned by Congress but contained to the Caribbean to avoid a real war. This localized conflict was much like the later *Phoney War* (*Sitzkrieg*—"inactive war") of 1939.

General George S. Patton Jr.; "Old Blood and Guts" (b. 1885)
He warned his men, "You're going to be up to your neck in blood and guts."
 Patton believed in his own personal reincarnations; and he means this literally (and literarily). His very, very long poem lists hypotheticals about his previous lives:

> *Through a Glass, Darkly*
> I have fought and strove and perished
> Countless times upon this star.
>
> . . .

I have battled for fresh mammoth,

. . .

Perhaps I stabbed our Savior
In His sacred helpless side.

. . .

Feel the pikes grow wet and slippery
When our Phalanx, Cyrus met.

. . .

Hear the rattle of the harness
Where the Persian darts bounced clear,
See their chariots wheel in panic
From the Hoplite's leveled spear.

. . .

Still more clearly as a Roman,
Can I see the Legion close,

. . .

And the lance ripped through my entrails
As on Crecy's field I lay.

. . .

Not bad for a general known for "the offensive spirit, the ruthless drive, and the will for victory in battle.... [who] brought the blitzkrieg concept to perfection," as Martin Blumenson put it.

General Eisenhower announced that Patton had been passed over as leader of the Normandy attack because of his physical abuse of troops suffering from shellshock. (Patton called shellshock "an invention of the Jews." You don't hear that today about PTSD.) Instead, before D-Day, he was assigned to command a (nonexistent) "Ghost Army" to mislead the Germans about the Normandy invasion site.

Patton had his initials etched on an ivory-handled Colt .45, which he carried everywhere.

Like Churchill, Patton was a drinking man; his cocktail of choice was the "Armored Diesel."

Napoleon (meaning *"Lion of Naples"*) *Bonaparte* (b. 1769)
In France, a law forbidding you to name your pig Napoleon is still on the books.

It's interesting that in *Animal Farm* George Orwell named his main character—a pig—*Napoleon*. Orwell's porcine Napoleon, however, was modeled on Stalin.

When it comes to animal names, the French take rules seriously. The name of a thoroughbred dog must begin with the alphabetic letter designated for the year of its whelping. And this now-resolutely-secular country only recently stopped requiring your legal name to be that of a saint.

Napoleon kept Leonardo's *Mona Lisa* in his bedroom. But this room's overall décor might not have been as nice. Some believe he was poisoned by arsenic in the wallpaper.

Napoleon's penis was given to a Corsican priest. *TIME* magazine later likened it to a "maltreated strip of buckskin shoelace." In 1977, a New Jersey urologist bought this item for $3000 and kept it under his bed. The doctor's family refused an offer of $100,000 for it.

Napoleon commissioned a "secure" military script—"Night Writing"—that could be read by touch. It never caught on, but later (1821) its military inventor Charles Barbier met Louis Braille and the duo developed a reading system for the blind.

Napoleon was afraid of open doors; a visitor had to edge through a narrow slit between door and frame.

There was a conspiracy to rescue him from his exile on St. Helena Island via a ship that could travel underwater.

Beethoven called his *Third Symphony* the "Sinfonia Eroica . . . composed to celebrate the memory of a great man," namely Napoleon.

A few fashion facts: Napoleon would purposely spill drinks or ink on a woman's dress if it displeased him, especially if he knew it was made of English fabric. Recall the other French emperor, Charlemagne, who was also partial to this particular practical joke, although with Napoleon it was political—to protect his country's textile industry.

His wife Josephine purchased nine hundred dresses annually and a thousand pairs of gloves to go with them. Most likely of French origin.

To make him easy to spot during a battle, Napoleon wore his *bicorne* hat with its "horns" (the two points designed to go front to back) sticking out sideways. Picture General Patton addressing his men with his hat visor turned 90 degrees off center.

Partly to prevent swordplay on horseback, his regime required traffic to travel on the right side of the road.

He cheated during card games, being one of those people who always have to win. While exiled, he played a lot of cards. He gave his name to several varieties of solitaire: Napoleon's Shoulder, Napoleon's Square, Little Napoleon, Napoleon at St. Helena, Napoleon's Flank. Look up the rules and try a few.

When he staged a royal rabbit hunt, more than a hundred hungry rabbits mobbed him. These rabbits were not afraid as his assistant had tamed them to make easier prey. Anyway, Napoleon fled.

Charles de Gaulle (b. 1890)
Palindrome: Napoleon was five foot six inches; de Gaulle was six foot five inches.

You may have used the corkscrew with arms that rise as the screw spirals down into the cork. The real name of the device is the "Charles de Gaulle" for its resemblance to the general lifting his arms in a V while addressing the public.

BARBARIAN
RAIDERS
(EUROPE AND THE EAST)

Alaric the Visigoth (a.k.a. ΛΛΛΡΕΙRS; *"ruler of all"* (reign c. 370–410 CE)
There were Goths and Goths. Always be scrupulous to distinguish
the Visigoths (western Goths) from the Ostrogoths (eastern Goths).

The Visigoth Alaric dreamt he was cruising Rome in a gold
chariot and being greeted as emperor by the locals. The vision gave
him big ideas.

In 408, an envoy from Rome sought a treaty with him, pointing
out the vast number of Romans he would gain as allies. Alaric
guffawed and replied with agro-political acumen: "The thicker the
hay, the easier mowed!" He sacked Rome in 410.

I'm sure you've often wondered who Stilicho was. You could have
taken the trouble to look him up on Wikipedia. Luckily for you,
I did. This Stilicho, a Vandal (i.e., from somewhere around modern
Poland), had beaten his rival Alaric in a couple of run-ins. But it was
Alaric who hit the jackpot by plundering Rome.

In the event of his death, he commanded that—along with the
best loot from his Roman adventure—he be buried in a river. Its
course was diverted for security reasons; workers on the gravesite
were subsequently killed to ensure eternal secrecy.

But what Alaric hadn't reckoned with was Merlin Burrows of
Merlin Burrows, Ltd. in North Yorkshire, who claims:

> We find anything that has been lost, forgotten or hidden with pin-point accuracy. We provide a full project management service to a bespoke level depending on the client requirements and the scope and parameters of the works required.

"Merlin Burrows" is a suspiciously good name for wizardry at digging things up. Be that as it may, the company announced in 2017: "Merlin Burrows has found and pin-pointed the exact location of the lost treasure and tomb of King Alaric." The statement added that "any interested party is warmly invited to direct enquiries to us at Merlin Burrows for further details."

Attila; The Wrath of God (fifth century)
As Attila put it, "Where I have passed, the grass will never grow."

Hungarians are still naming their sons "Attila," which means "little father."

The Huns, who are from the Steppes of Central Asia, are all about horsemanship.

The Roman historian Ammianus, who should know (being their contemporary), calls them *prodigiose deformes et pandi, ut bipedes existimes bestias*—"so extremely hideous and bent over that you might take them for two-legged animals." (In the Hunnish horse-based culture this might have passed for a compliment.)

Meeting Attila in person in the year 449, the Roman envoy Priscus called him short and snub-nosed. Don't confuse this with cute. "To see him was to quake at his gaze."

Huns, in fact, strove for a special look. They might, for instance, press an infant's head between pieces of wood to lengthen its cranium into a cone. *Il faut souffrir pour être belle.* Since foul weather gear hadn't been invented, they rubbed grease into their hair and skin to make rain slide off. Go ahead and shudder, but keep in mind Coco Chanel's dictum, "Fashion changes, but style endures."

Attila probably killed his brother Bleda to allow himself solo rule over his large tribe. As leaders go, Attila was not really the Chaucerian *parfit gentil knyght*. But then we've already seen the ruthless practices of wannabe kings, and all for a crown—a leaky "hat" that lets the rain in. Hun society was a kind of necrocracy, where your rank was determined by the number people you'd killed. Your *curriculum vitae* was a *curriculum mortis*.

Huns trained their horses to use their huge hooves and teeth against enemies. But a horse served many functions. A Hun could heat his own meal of raw meat on its warm back. (Alternatively he might warm up his food between his own thighs.) Horse milk was a basic beverage, but it remains the Mongolian national drink, *airag*, to this day. The Huns only rarely had recourse to horse blood.

In 453, Attila died of nosebleed. An ignoble death: he never had any Hunnish Valkyries, beautiful maidens to select him for a Hunnish Valhalla. But he did receive due honor. He was buried in a golden coffin, inside a silver one, inside an iron one, in a hidden, custom-made tributary of a river. For extra security, all the men who helped inter him were killed, and the penalty for potential disinterment would be death.

Déjà vu? Yes, or more specifically, *déjà lu* ("already read") in the Alaric entry above. In fact, this river business sounds fishy in its resemblance to Alaric's burial. Maybe the two tales were conflated or confused? Or maybe Attila's was a copycat case. But don't fault me for sloppy mixed-up reportage. At least in legends, rivers were popular royal resting places. Or maybe the practice originated with Gilgamesh, who wanted the Euphrates River diverted over his grave.

What we can count on is that Attila's followers paid him further homage by hacking off their hair and killing poultry for blood to daub on their faces. Greek women in mourning, after all, had pulled out their hair at the death of a loved one. I'll check whether psychiatrists have a name for it. (I checked: Yes—*trichotillomania*, where treatments include habit-reversal training, cognitive therapy, and acceptance and commitment therapy.)

Genghis Khan (d. 1227)

Another Hunnic ruler, Genghis Khan was born "Temujin," meaning "iron man" or "blacksmith," before an *iron man* was a triathlon. He became "Genghis Kahn" when his tribe chose him as Mongol chief.

Here's what you want in the delivery room: to be born with your fist clenched around a blood clot. Did they rush tiny Temujin to the NICU? No, and that was good, since thrombolysis might have interfered with his "future-ruler" omen.

Genghis had a trade agreement with the Shah of Persia for mutual use of the Silk Road. And when the first Mongol traders to use it were killed, Genghis made Persia pay. Violence was the essence of the Mongol zeitgeist.

You didn't want to mess with Genghis. 1) His mounted Mongol archers were unequalled, and 2) he operated The Yam, not a vegetable institution but an intelligence network of long-distance riders. Mongol rule extended from the Pacific Ocean to the Mediterranean.

In aid of conquest, he had no scruples about killing women and children. He simply wiped out any non-compliant region. Nor was the Mongol M.O. a merciful M.O. Three practices: Twist an enemy's back to snap the spine. Inject hot silver into his bodily orifices. Wrap him in a rug and ride over him with a horse, or two.

As in Attila's world, the horse was a full-service amenity, which he came in handy during bouts of paranoia. When a certain mountain was out to get him, he appeased it with mare's milk, a commodity which also brought luck when applied to a battlefield. His fortune failed in horseback hunting, however, when he was thrown to his death. Too bad for him: today's equestrian trainers know that "learning how to fall off a horse is a key skill."

The Mongols added an equine twist to imperial tomb treatment. Genghis was buried with forty horses. A thousand horses trampled on his grave to conceal the site, which for a change was not beneath a bespoke river. And who needs a labor-intensive river-burial if there's a stampede available to conceal the site? Naturally, all the gravediggers—and all those who saw the funeral procession—were murdered and their murderers were murdered for good measure. Rigorous reverence forbids anyone to look for his bones, so don't bother. And don't call Merlin Burrows either.

Genghis Kahn left such a lasting mark on history that, seven centuries later, the Soviets tried to snuff out Mongolian nationalists by expunging Genghis from textbooks and even forbidding the utterance of his name—fat chance of that.

Tamerlaine; The Sword of Islam; "Timur the Lame" (b. 1336)
He was a Turco-Mongol conqueror, native of Transoxiana, what today is Uzbekistan. "Tamerlaine" means "iron," surely derived from the same root as Genghis's "Temujin." Iron is a perennially popular metal for a ruler's name. Stalin ("man of steel," you recall) knew, of course, that—due to its carbon content—steel was a thousand times stronger than iron. Further research on this fact, however, informs us: "You don't need to consume steel as part of your diet." But never mind that. What with the iron, we can assume Tamerlaine was not anemic.

Why you should have heard of Tamerlaine: not because of Christopher Marlowe's noted play *Tamburlaine*, but because he murdered about 5 percent of the world population of his time.

The slaughters were in the name of Islam. "Holy war" is what we often hear from egocentric empire-builders. He ordered every warrior to bring him the heads of a couple of Christians.

Tamerlaine was a tactical wizard: When the Indians attacked with elephants in armor, he deployed camels carrying burning oil. The Indian elephants turned around and trampled their own Indian army.

Tamerlaine is buried in the Gur Amir mausoleum in Samarkand, beneath a six-foot-long black jade slab, at the time supposedly the world's biggest stone.

Archaeologists exhumed him in 1941 (the corpse's maimed leg proved they had the actual crippled king). This disinterment took place despite the customary exhumation-curse: his grave inscription said, "Whoever opens my tomb shall unleash an invader more terrible than I," and before you snort in contempt, note that Hitler invaded Russia two days after his body was dug up.

SCIENTISTS

Pythagoras (b. circa 570 BC)
He's been named "the Father of Vegetarianism." But there was one vegetable he kept away from—understandably, when we learn that beans enclose the souls of the departed.

Archimedes (b. 287 BC)
I've catalogued plenty of braggarts, especially in the despot category. But when Archimedes said, "Give me a place to stand, and I shall move the Earth with it," he wasn't posturing but touting the power of the fulcrum.

Besides, if he didn't move the earth, he did break new ground. He invented not only the principle of the *lever* but also:

The *Claw of Archimedes*: a giant grapple to pick up invading ships and capsize them. I hear you sniggering, but twenty-first-century engineers who modeled and tested the giant gadget were able to topple and sink a mock-up of a Roman ship.

Archimedes' screw: a manually wound cylinder containing blades that raise water.

Pi: he figured out the numerical ratio.

Early calculus: Determining the area under a curve. Hitherto only angular shapes could be calculated.

What he's known for is his *Eureka!* in the bathtub where Archimedes sought to prove an allegedly "gold" crown was an adulterated fake. His assay (himself in a bathtub) revealed the principle of specific gravity. Perhaps apocryphal is that when he uttered his famous cry, he ran from tub to town, still nude, with his news. Please don't use the cliché "Eureka moment."

Copernicus (b. 1473)

His personal element on the periodic table is Copernicium (Cn.), atomic number 112 and exceptionally radioactive.

He thought the planets, including earth, circled some even bigger object, but he didn't go so far as Galileo, who would posit the sun as hub.

Copernicus was buried in the Polish Archcathedral Basilica of the Assumption of the Blessed Virgin Mary and St. Andrew, where the church's name is longer than his skeleton and where in 2004 archaeologists verified his identity with DNA found in a book he'd owned.

Galileo (b. 1564)

This just in (really) from CNN: "A prized manuscript in the University of Michigan library that was believed to have been written by the famed Italian astronomer Galileo Galilei is a forgery, the university said . . . likely written by the notorious Italian forger Tobia Nicotra. . . . It purported to show notes recording Galileo's discovery of Jupiter's four moons."

If Archimedes had his *Eureka*, Galileo has his own famous phrase: *Eppur si muove*. After the church forced him to retract his notion that the earth circles the sun and is not the center of the universe, he allegedly muttered, *Eppur si muove*—i.e., whatever they claim, "the earth *does* move [around the sun]."

Galileo was charged with flouting Scripture and sentenced to a weekly reading of *Seven Penitential Psalms*. His conviction stood for three-and-a-half centuries, until 1979, when Pope John Paul reopened the case and declared the verdict erroneous.

Galileo was an expert lutenist. A true Renaissance Man.

In other musical news, one of the Indigo Girls' hit songs is "Galileo" (1992). Selected lyrics: *Galileo's head was on the block / The crime was lookin' up the truth.*

You can see Galileo's middle finger in a Florence museum.Still flipping the bird at the churchmen.

But that's not the osteological end for Galileo, because today you can own a *Nylabone Beef Extreme Galileo Bone* for your dog: According to their literature, "Galileo once used a bone to illustrate his theory about the strength of materials in proportion to their size, and we put his studies to work to create the Galileo Chew Toy!"

Johannes Kepler (b. 1571)

Kepler served as Imperial Mathematician to the Holy Roman Emperor. Also, he discovered the laws of planetary motion, for instance the Law of Harmonies, whereby the ratio of the squares of the periods of any two planets is equal to the ratio of the cubes of their average distances from the sun. I'm sure this equation is as valuable to you as it is to me.

Top achievement: he invented eyeglasses.

René Descartes (b. 1596)

The *philosophe* Descartes confessed: "Seeing cross-eyed women, I felt more inclined to love them than others."

In 1619, Descartes had dreams showing him that no man could tell what was real and what was merely human perception. Coming up with that concept itself proved he existed; in other words, *cogito ergo sum* (I think, therefore I am).

He took the house arrest of his contemporary Galileo as a cautionary tale and decided to keep mum about his own heliocentric notions.

Geometry students can thank him for the Cartesian coordinates system, which introduced the relationship of geometry to algebra. He said there was no such thing as a vacuum. His fellow-*philosophe* Pascal, however, did believe in vacuums, and Descartes wrote that Pascal had "too much vacuum in his head." I'm no logician, but doesn't that contradict Descartes' own denial of vacuums? The abstract of a paper by Joseph Zepeda simplifies Descartes' position: "Descartes is notorious for holding a strong anti-vacuist position . . . we cannot infer from the fact that Descartes argues, e.g., that something is a superfluous theoretical entity, that he admits that entity's coherence." You can see why it's called an *abstract*.

Descartes' personal motto came from Ovid: *Bene qui latuit bene vixit.* Lie low and live well. He moved around and concealed his addresses. Hence arose the rumor that he was a spy for the Catholic Church. His lifelong religious faith is weird for a proponent of logic—until you consider the deep roots of a Jesuit education.

Galileo isn't the only one with bones in a museum. Descartes' cranium is in the *Musée de l'Homme* in Paris.

Isaac Newton (b. December 25, 1642)

This book is supposed to report *obscure* items concerning renowned individuals, so forgive my mentioning a Newtonian discovery you already know by heart:

The attractive force (F) between two objects is equal to G times the product of their masses (m1m2) divided by the square of the distance between them (r2); that is, $F = Gm1m2/r2$. The value of G, of course, is $(6.6743 \pm 0.00015) \times 10{-}11$ m3 kg-1 s-2.

(And if *you* happen to be the alert reader who found typos in a formula in my previous book, please proofread these data for me.)

Prompted by Edmond Halley, Newton wrote his *Philosophiae Naturalis Principia Mathematica* on planetary motions. Unfortunately, the Royal Society had spent its budget on a non-bestseller called *The History of Fishes*, so Halley subsidized the publication of his colleague's book.

Newton gave us the Newtonian reflector to show a prism's visible spectrum. One day, in what he called experimentation and I call masochism/lunacy, "I took a bodkin and put it betwixt my eye and the bone as near to the backside of my eye as I could, and on pressing my eye with the end of it, there appeared several white, dark, and colored circles." He wrote the law of cooling, gave us an estimation of the speed of sound, and provided the principles of calculus, about which he charged Leibniz with plagiarism.

During his tenure as Master of the Royal Mint, forgerers were not only hanged but drawn and quartered.

Newton was a father of modern science; as just one more example, take his cure for the plague, using a toad suspended by the legs in a chimney for three days, which at last vomited up the earth with various insects in it, onto a dish of yellow wax, and shortly after died. Combining powdered toad with the excretions and serum made into lozenges and worn about the affected area drove away the contagion and drew out the poison.

We can think of Newton as the epitome of a rational scientist, but think again.

He was an alchemist and wanted to isolate the philosopher's stone, the fabled mineral that could transmute base metals into gold. He chronicled his work in a secret coded log. Some claim his experiments resulted in the mercury poisoning discovered in analysis of his hair.

He was also absorbed by bible research and spent more time on religious work than on what we call science.

Newton predicted the date for the end of the world: "And the days of short-lived Beasts being put for the years of lived [sic] kingdoms, the period of 1260 days, if dated from the complete conquest of the three kings AC 800, will end AC 2060. It may end later, but I see no reason for its ending sooner."

He also kept a catalog of his confessed sins:

> "Threatning [sic] my father and mother Smith to burne them and the house over them."
> "Eating an apple at Thy house."
> "Stealing cherry cobs from Eduard Storer."
> "Robbing my mothers [sic] box of plums and sugar."
> "Making pies on Sunday night."
> "Punching my sister."
> "Making a feather while on Thy day."
> "Denying that I made it."
> "Making a mousetrap on Thy day."
> "Squirting water on Thy day."

Neil deGrasse Tyson calls Newton "The smartest person ever to walk the face of this earth . . . He discovered the laws of motion, the laws of gravity, the laws of optics. Then he turned twenty-six."

Edmond Halley (b. 1656)
Halley was pondering celestial motions, particularly those of comets, when he consulted an introvert mathematician at Cambridge University named Isaac Newton.

This encounter was ordained in the stars. As mentioned, it was Halley who got Newton to record his theories in what became the *Philosophiae Naturalis Principia* on planetary motions; Halley wrote a Latin ode for his foreword to the book.

Halley ran afoul of church teachings when he denied that the world was created on October 23 at 9 a.m. in 4004 BCE: On the premise that the ocean water started out non-saline, the seas would have needed to be around for 100,000,000 years (not 1200) for salt to leach from the lands to its present proportion in seawater. He also suggested that the flood Noah coped with had been caused by a comet's shock waves.

In the recreation sphere, Halley gave the visiting Tsar Peter the Great a drunken wheelbarrow ride.

Louis Pasteur (b. 1822)
Medical: When he was developing a rabies vaccine, Pasteur limited his trials to rabbits. But when a boy was bitten by a rabid dog, he broke protocol and vaccinated the child, saving countless future lives.

Commercial: He salvaged the French silk industry by diagnosing and culling diseased silkworms.

Charles Darwin (b. 1809)
A Darwin bestseller was *The Formation of Vegetable Mould Through the Action of Worms, With Observations on Their Habits.*

Darwin was president of the "Glutton Club," created to consume "strange flesh" like armadillo and a rodent weighing twenty pounds. He drew the line at brown owls.

His would-be medical career came to a dead end when he found that blood horrified him. His father's reaction: "You care for nothing but shooting, dogs and rat catching, and you will be a disgrace to yourself and all your family."

His grandfather had written in his *Zoonomia*: "Would it be too bold to imagine, that all warm-blooded animals have arisen from one living filament?"

Darwin believed, "A scientific man ought to have no wishes, no affections, a mere heart of stone." Before proposing marriage to his first cousin, he wrote down the pros and cons—tidily, in two columns. Reasons against marriage included loss of educated conversation, time for himself, and freedom in general.

In his late teens, an emancipated slave taught him taxidermy. (The future held specimens for him that the young Darwin didn't dream of.)

In Darwin we have another scientist rehabilitated by the church, which addressed him thus:

"Charles Darwin: 200 years from your birth, the Church of England owes you an apology for misunderstanding you and, by getting our first reaction wrong, encouraging others to misunderstand you still."

Gregor (Czech Řehoř) Mendel (b. 1822)

For a free education, Mendel entered a monastic order in the (prettily alliterative) Margraviate of Moravia; he later became its abbot. We owe it to the Augustinian monks that Mendel became the "Father of Genetics," where his research on peas demonstrated the 3:1 inheritance of dominant and recessive traits.

Mme. Maria Skłodowska Curie (b. 1867)

Marie's mother and sister both died when she was a child. Because their Catholic God was so callous as to let them die, she renounced religion.

Since women were barred from universities, she taught herself chemistry at the Warsaw Museum of Industry and Agriculture. Studying in her frigid Paris lodging, she had to wear all her garments layered on simultaneously.

At one point she had to hide at a friend's house to escape the crowds scandalized by her affair with a younger married man.

Mme. Curie was the first woman whose body was placed in the Paris Panthéon (in 1995). Her body is wrapped in three layers of lead to protect visitors from radiation.

Alfred Nobel (b.1833)

Nobel invented dynamite. A nitroglycerin explosion in the Nobel family factory killed his brother and four others.

At the time, most oil wells used Nobel's gelignite, making him rich. But he was called "merchant of death." He improved his image when he put his fortune into philanthropy. In his own words, "I am a misanthrope, but exceedingly benevolent." Several winners of the Nobel Prize have declined it. Jean-Paul Sartre refused it out of aversion to being "institutionalized." In 1964 the USSR compelled Boris Paternak to turn it down. Hitler ruled that no German could accept a Nobel Prize.

His namesake element, Nobelium, first produced in 1956 and known as *unbinilium* pending final naming, is a synthetic substance created by nuclear fission.

James Watson (b. 1928)

The University of Chicago awarded Watson a scholarship when he was only fifteen years old.

Watson was so unwoke he was downright comatose; he was a poster-child for prejudice. He viewed good looks as one of a woman's main assets. Of Rosalind Franklin—his overlooked colleague in the discovery of DNA—he said:

> By choice she did not emphasize her feminine qualities. Though her features were strong, she was not unattractive and might have been quite stunning had she taken even a mild interest in

clothes. This she did not. There was never lipstick to contrast with her straight black hair, while at the age of thirty-one her dresses showed all the imagination of English blue-stocking adolescents.

To him she was merely "Rosy," who didn't really count. He and Crick plagiarized her pictures of DNA without crediting her.

Other aspects of personal appearance also mattered to him: "Whenever you interview fat people, you feel bad, because you know you're not going to hire them." "Some anti-Semitism is justified." "There's a difference on the average between blacks and whites in IQ tests. I would say the difference is genetic." He said that if it ever became possible to isolate a "gay gene," abortion should be legal. He checked all the bigotry boxes.

His opinion of female scientists: "I think having all these women around makes it more fun for the men, but they're probably less effective." Oddly, however, his own wife, Elizabeth, as police chief of Houston, was certainly more than a pretty face.

Blaming others for judging him as a kind of "unperson" for his racism, he auctioned off his Nobel medal for four million dollars.

Francis Crick (b. 1916)
Unlike his American colleague, the British Crick was a buoyant extrovert. Example: the head of the lab where he pursued his doctorate couldn't wait to ditch the garrulous, rowdy young man.

While working together on an unrelated grant, Watson and Crick started to slack off on the research stipulated in their grant and focus their work on their own DNA project.

Like many close relationships, Watson and Crick's was bumpy. Watson's reaction to the opening words of Crick's book: "I have never seen Francis Crick in a modest mood." (Perhaps true.)

He charged Crick with "widespread dissemination of a book which grossly invades my privacy, and I have yet to hear an argument which adequately excuses such a violation of friendship." Crick in turn warned Watson he'd sue him for libel; due to opposition from Crick and another scientist, Harvard revoked the publication contract for the book.

Samuel Morse (b. 1791)
He called his children Dot and Dash.

His last words in Morse code: "Greeting and thanks to the Telegraph fraternity throughout the world. Glory to God in the Highest, on Earth Peace, Goodwill to men."

Thomas Alva Edison; "Al" (b. 1847)
Speaking of Morse, Thomas Edison proposed to his wife in Morse code.

Edison was afraid of the dark (though I'm not saying this was a factor in his invention of the first practical light bulb). Even—or especially—on his deathbed he required that every light in the house be lit. But Edison didn't invent lightbulb technology; Humphry Davy had already produced incandescent light.

Edison's teachers said he was "too stupid to learn anything." He was fired from his first two jobs for being "non-productive."

Edison would sometimes hold two metal balls which would drop noisily and wake him if he started to doze off. Today's consumer, on the other hand, can choose the *Driver Fatigue Monitor* for $199, and I think the (cheaper) pair of falling balls would be the better option in general, except when you have a gas pedal at your feet.

His first phrase on the newly invented phonograph: "Mary had a little lamb." To continue the child motif, he installed recordings (on wax cylinders) inside a "speaking" doll. The ghastly voice issuing from holes in her chest terrified the target consumer. The toy bombed.

Indeed, not all Edison's projects became commercial successes. He informed the press that he was developing a "spirit phone" to communicate with the dead. Its algorithm translated atmospheric "life units" from the deceased.

He proposed concrete furniture as cheaper and more durable than wood; it could be polished or even have a fake wood veneer. Like the doll, the concept didn't fly.

When Edison died, the president asked citizens to turn off their lights briefly to pay their respects.

Alexander Graham Bell (b. 1847)

Bell's wife and his mother were deaf, and he came up with various audio contrivances, leading in 1876 to a telephone. He spurned this device as a waste of his time and wouldn't even own one. (My comment is *O tempora, o mores*, by which I mean things have changed.) After President Garfield was shot and Bell invented a proto-metal-detector, neither did he realize how crucial its development would be for future airline concerns.

But Bell was prescient about genetics. He tried to develop multiple births in sheep. Not quite like cloning a Dolly, but he did get twins and triplets.

Reminiscent of Edison's death, telephone service was suspended in all of North America during Bell's funeral.

Gugliemo Marconi (b. 1874)

We should heap gratitude on Marconi, who invented the radio in 1943.

A member of the Italian aristocracy, Marconi was a staunch Fascist who said, "I reclaim the honor of being the first fascist in the field of radiotelegraphy." He was at least a bit of a wit.

You sailors know that a boat's triangular Marconi rig was named for him as the wires that fix the mast in place resembled those on radio masts.

Marconi too was recognized at his death, in his case by two minutes of radio silence.

Nikola Tesla (b. 1856)

Tesla's first name is *Српска ћирилиц* in Serbian, and only Serbs know how that turned into his English name.

CNN reports (2022) that there's a Tesla owner who "has his car key implanted in his hand." If you're a Luddite, you call this the beginning of the end of civilization.

Tesla loved: the number three.

He hated: circular items; the feel of hair; all jewelry, especially pearls; and fat people. He sacked an overweight employee and sent another one home to change her outfit and get rid of her pearls.

If you want a brain like Tesla's, curl and clench your toes tightly a hundred times daily (Marc Seifer tells us Tesla performed this exercise to boot up his morning brainpower). This practice is useful if your aim, like his, is to receive sudden visions of things waiting for you to invent.

His contemporary, Arthur Brisbane, describes Tesla's "very big hands" and "remarkably big" thumbs.

Tesla worked on a frequency-oscillating device which, inconveniently for neighbors, also delivered small shocks to nearby buildings. He put Mark Twain, who suffered chronic constipation, onto this "earthquake machine," which solved the problem immediately.

Max Planck (b. 1858)

Planck's university professor advised him not to study physics theory because there was nothing new to discover.

Planck did come up with quantum theory, but he was also a polymath who nearly became a professional pianist: he and Einstein played together in chamber-music concerts. Unfortunately, Planck was blessed/cursed with perfect pitch, which interfered with his pleasure in hearing music.

Another reason to admire him is his argument with Hitler against firing Jewish scientists. Predictably, this attitude got him into trouble. An "Aryan Physics" cadre accused Planck of plotting to block "German" scientists from professorships; the Gestapo conducted zealous, and you might say overzealous, background checks on him (later they killed his son Erwin). And the periodical *Das Schwarze Korps* called both Planck and Einstein "bacteria carriers."

Wright Brothers (Wilbur and Orville, b. 1867 and 1871)

The young Wright boys were given a toy helicopter composed of bamboo, cork, paper, and an elastic propellor. Modeled on this item, they built a two-seater version with human dimensions: the "Wright Flyer."

Neither boy could spare the time to finish high school; Wilbur additionally claimed he didn't have time for *both* airplanes and marriage. As for Orville, his sister's companionship was enough, though he deemed her eventual marriage such a betrayal that he shunned her until she was on her deathbed. He did take his octogenarian father for a flight (less than one minute and under four hundred feet above the ground).

The subsequent use of planes for bombing devastated the Wrights: "We underestimated man's capacity to hate and to corrupt good means for an evil end."

Aboard the first lunar flight, Neil Armstrong's suit had fragments from the 1903 Wright plane stitched into it.

Albert Einstein (b. 1879)

Don't let your baby's delayed speaking dismay you unduly. The toddler Einstein didn't talk till he was at least three—to complain about the temperature of his soup.

Like many prodigies, he loathed school, to the point that he considered pretending to be mentally ill.

Einstein would not wear socks because his big toes punched through the fabric. He preferred his sandals, and if he misplaced them, he borrowed his wife's Elsa's sling-backs. Maybe she didn't mind lending her shoes, but she certainly minded lending her husband for numerous adulteries—which Einstein defended, saying "one should do what one enjoys, and won't harm anyone else." He was a notorious philanderer.

Also, and famously, he more than mistreated his first wife Mileva Marić. Walter Isaacson reports his regulations:

CONDITIONS

You will make sure:

1. That my clothes and laundry are kept in good order;
2. That I will receive my three meals regularly in my room;
3. That my bedroom and study are kept neat, and especially that my desk is left for my use only.

You will renounce all personal relations with me insofar as they are not completely necessary for social reasons. Specifically, you will forego:
1. My sitting at home with you;
2. My going out or travelling with you.

You will obey the following points in your relations with me:
1. You will not expect any intimacy from me, nor will you reproach me in any way;
2. You will stop talking to me if I request it;
3. You will leave my bedroom or study immediately without protest if I request it.

We talked above about Frederick the Great's dictum that *a crown is merely a hat that lets the rain in*. As befits a king of science, Einstein (relates Peter Bucky) removed his hat during a rain shower (because the water didn't harm his hair as much as it did his hat). Besides, a previous experiment had demonstrated the precise drying time of his hair.

Apropos of rain, my father (at the Philadelphia train station) observed Einstein standing in the rain a couple of feet from the roofed area of the platform—too deep in conversation to bother to take a step sideways into shelter.

Einstein was an addicted smoker who picked cigarette butts off the ground and wadded the leftover tobacco leaves into the bowl of his pipe. When he finally stopped smoking, he still kept the stem of a pipe clenched between his teeth.

His happiest possession was his violin, "Lina."

Einstein said, "When I examine myself and my methods of thought, I come close to the conclusion that the gift of fantasy has meant more to me than my talent for absorbing positive knowledge." As a teenager Einstein repudiated Germany as his country. Nor, however, did he completely approve of American politics. The FBI, trying to prove he was a Communist, amassed a massive file on this dangerous radical. And of course, anti-racism is always fishy (Einstein belonged to the NAACP).

Scientific bagatelles:
As a physicist-cum-ladies' man, here's one way Einstein described the concept of relativity: "When you are courting a nice girl an hour seems like a second. When you sit on a red-hot cinder a second seems like an hour. That's relativity."

The theory of special relativity came to Einstein while he was dreaming about cows being electrocuted; and one doesn't immediately see how that relates to relativity.

Two other dream-triggered discoveries:
DNA—Watson dreamed of a pair of snakes intertwined in a helix.

Elias Howe struggled to design a sewing-machine needle. Hitherto (in hand-held needles) the eye was at the blunt end—where your fingers grasp it, unless you're a moron and masochist who tries to hold it by the tip. In a dream, Elias failed to meet an impatient king's deadline for building a sewing machine. Elias's executioners wielded spears (he noticed *in extremis*) with slits at the pointed end, as dream-spears often feature. Had he known Latin or Greek, Elias would have cried "QED" or even "Eureka." As an apprentice in a textile mill, a wool-carding shop, and a clockmaking atelier, however, he surely had no time for classical study.

When Einstein and Niels Bohr argued over quantum theory. Einstein disputed that the functions of nature were based on random probability. Bohr won the debate.

> Einstein: "God does not play dice with the universe."
> Bohr: "Stop telling God what to do."
> Stephen Hawking, retrospective referee: "God not only plays dice. He also throws the dice where they cannot be seen."
> (The Carlsberg brewery gave Bohr a house with beer piped in, which would have been useless to Einstein, who drank only wine and cognac, sparingly.)

As the astute reader will guess, Einsteinium, the 99th element on the periodic table, is named in Einstein's honor, even though it was not in his field of endeavor.

An aside: Dreams and elements bring us to Dmitri Mendeleev's design of the periodic table, which he envisioned during a twenty-minute nap. He sketched a diagram immediately, a vital practice for an eel-like dream: after conceiving part of his poem *Kubla Khan* during an opium dream, Coleridge immediately committed it to paper. He claimed he would have completed the poem if a tradesman from the town of Porlock hadn't disturbed him.

In Einstein's physical brain, the lobes governing mathematics and spatial sense were unusually large. In 1955 Dr. Thomas Harvey purloined the brain and put it in a pair of mason jars. Don't confuse this physician with the celebrated seventh-century William Harvey, who discovered the basic process of blood circulation in the heart, "the citadel of the body."

Subcategory: Two Imposters

Clark Rockefeller, actually *Christian Karl Gerhartsreiter* (b. 1961)
His fake surname wormed him into social circles, netting him a rich wife. Unwisely, he tried to kidnap his young daughter (his ex-wife had custody). He ended up in custody himself. He was later convicted of murder in a case too byzantine to detail here.

Anna Vadimovna Sorokina (b. 1991)
Another poseur—pseudonym Anna Delvey.
    You may know of Anna Sorokin. While in prison, she was recreated in the 2022 docuseries *Inventing Anna.* So I'll note only that when she became a media phenom, she tried, ever-mercenary, to sell to the press the identity of her (allegedly famous) ex-boyfriend, asking price $10K.

TECHNOLOGY

Bill Gates (b. 1955)

After the teenaged Gates coded a Tic-Tac-Toe game, high school administrators made him responsible for the school's scheduling program, where he made sure his own classes had a "disproportionate number of interesting girls."

A Harvard drop-out, Gates got a Harvard degree another way: an honorary one.

With the celebrated Bill and Melinda Gates Foundation, his philanthropic gifts total over $50 billion.

Steve Jobs (b. 1955)

Steve Jobs's father, Abdulfattah Jandali, was Syrian.

To relax while at work, Jobs soaked his feet in the toilet. Probably nothing to do with his idiosyncratic and weird way of walking.

Believing vegetarians had no body odor, he figured he could skip showers. His supervisor at Atari had to switch him to night duty.

For reasons unknown, Jobs leased a car so he could drive without a license plate. Probably something to do with illegal parking.

For years he repudiated his daughter and never provided for her; oddly, he named two computers after her—the Lisa I and Lisa II.

We begin to wonder how likable Jobs was. He could be unpleasant in the workplace. Walter Isaacson reports on an interview where he asked a job candidate whether he was a virgin or had taken LSD—then mocked his discomfited victim when he tried to respond.

He assigned a group of workers to practice opening boxes of new products to evaluate the delight the buyer would experience.

Jobs could not write code.

Steve Jobs's signature black turtlenecks came exclusively from an exclusive Japanese designer.

His girlfriends included Joan Baez and Diane Keaton.

Jobs chose alternative medicine to treat his cancer—a choice, according to biographer Isaacson, that he later lamented.

As if he himself were delighted by a new experience (death), his last words were: "Oh, wow. Oh, wow. Oh, wow."

Elon Musk (b. 1971)

Tesla CEO Musk fathered twins and triplets—all boys. With a different wife he named another son X Æ A-12 Musk, and here's how to say it: "x-ash-a-12".

Before Elon was in his teens, a magazine bought his video game *Blastar*. (He did know a good product name.)

Musk's Stanford PhD program lasted two days. He had a corporation to found.

He bought Wet Nellie, James Bond's Lotus Esprit submarine-car; the car had been mislaid after the movie and was found swaddled in a blanket in Long Island.

Told he was officially the world's wealthiest person, he replied, "How strange," possibly reflecting on his Tesla salary of $1 per annum.

Jeff Bezos (b. 1964)

At age four, Jeffrey Preston Jorgensen became Jeff *Bezos*—the surname of his Cuban stepfather.

The tot Bezos, considering his baby crib beneath his dignity, took a screwdriver and disassembled it.

Bezos was an entrepreneur from the start. In his mid-teens he founded the *Dream Institute*, a summer learning camp for tweens.

Amazon's original name was *Cadabra*. When he decided this sounded too much like "cadaver," he hit on *Amazon* to imply his bookstore was like the world's biggest river.

Bezos's *Two Pizza Rule*: invite only the number of meeting attendees that two pizzas can feed.

Atop a mountain on his Texan property, he wants to engineer a five-hundred-foot-high ten-thousand-year clock with a century hand. An even loftier enterprise was Bezos's spaceship *Blue Origin*, conceived because Earth needed it for extraterrestrial resources.

In 2020 he became the first person in modern history to accumulate a fortune of over $200 billion.

Mark Zuckerberg (b. 1984)
In high school his top subject was the classics—he still prefers Virgil's *Aeneid* to most other books.

He met his wife in a restroom at a Harvard fraternity fête.

Harvard authorities put an end to Zuckerberg's Face-Mash application, and you can see why, since its function was posting photos of pairs of students where viewers voted which was better-looking.

His next project was Facebook, and it infuriated three students who claimed he had stolen features from their own site, Harvard-Connection.com. Zuckerberg tried, to no avail, to keep *The Harvard Crimson* from reporting on the dispute. I'd say his concern suggests his denial was without merit.

Zuckerberg is red/green color-blind, hence Facebook's blue logo.

Unlike Steve Jobs, he did eat meat—but only if *he* had personally killed the animal. He's reported to have used a laser gun on a goat.

PRIMATOLOGISTS

As you might guess, this is a very short section.

Jane Goodall (b. 1934)
She said that as a child she had fallen for Tarzan "although he married the wrong Jane, the wretched man."

At twenty-six, Goodall made a breakthrough: she found that chimpanzees used tools. Scientists had believed that man was the only toolmaker. She was also the first to discover that chimpanzees are carnivorous. In response to these findings, Louis Leakey stated, "We must now redefine *man*, redefine *tool*, or accept chimpanzees as human."

She earned a Cambridge University PhD, having been accepted there despite lacking an undergraduate degree.

She married her photographer from *National Geographic* (which funded her).

Goodall was one of the female "Trimates" in primate research. The other two were Dian Fossey (gorillas) and Birute Galdikas (orangutans).

Dian Fossey; Nyiramachabelli "solitary mountain woman" Swahili
(b. 1932)
Originally an occupational therapist, she said her experience with autism in children helped her gorilla work.

People heading for the wilderness occasionally had prophylactic appendectomies. After her operation, Fossey said Louis Leakey had ordered it only as proof she was serious about her research.

Fossey distinguished different gorillas by their nose wrinkles.

She was killed by a machete-strike to her face, thought to be the work of anti-conservation poachers; her American assistant was another suspect. The case is still unsolved.

MEDICINE

Florence Nightingale, Statistician; *"The Lady with the Lamp"* (b. 1820)
I didn't expect to find Florence Nightingale described as a statistician. What about the gently-bred Victorian angel of mercy, bathing foreheads of soldiers wounded in the Crimea?

Her group of professional statisticians measured military mortality and found that of the eighteen thousand killed in the Crimean War, sixteen thousand died of disease: the resulting "Nightingale Rose Diagram" was neither a floral cultivation chart nor a needlepoint pattern but a mortality-rate mapping.

You look at it and say, "A pie chart. Big deal." In point of fact, smarty pants, it involves the x (sin) and y (cos) components of the aspect and a few other things and shows the output as a vector. And you may also be surprised to hear that, "With small data sets, directions can be binned." From their rooster-comb-shaped graphs, these diagrams are also called *coxcombs*.

But Nightingale viewed her real role as a feminist reformer, claiming women should transcend domestic tedium and use their brains, particularly for bettering the lot of oppressed women. She wanted to legalize prostitution, institute female employment rights, and fight hunger in India. Her novella *Cassandra* lobbies for a woman "who will resume [sic], in her own soul all the sufferings of her race." And God was her witness: "Jesus Christ raised women above the condition of mere slaves, mere ministers to the passions of the man."

The prim-and-proper caregiver also understood the soldiers' morale: according to the History Press, Queen Victoria wanted to send them *eau de cologne*, but Florence suggested "a little gin would more popular."

Nightingale managed London's *Institution for the Care of Sick Gentlewomen in Distressed Circumstances*, which was the forerunner of a non-religious nurses' training school.

If you take the *Nightingale Pledge* nowadays, I doubt it starts: *I solemnly pledge myself before God and in the presence of this assembly to pass my life in purity and to practice my profession faithfully. I shall abstain from whatever is deleterious and mischievous . . .*

Florence Nightingale caught "Crimean fever"—perhaps brucellosis—which plagued her from age thirty-seven on.

Sigmund Freud (b. 1856)

Freud investigated eel sex habits. Safe to assume this research choice was related to his obsession with the male organ.

You may already know that for Freud all women were fundamentally damaged by penis envy. As for lesbians, they were more or less mentally ill. Gay men's inevitable neuroses, on the other hand, troubled Freud not at all: men, at least are moral beings. Unlike a female, a boy—thanks to castration complex—acquires virtue lest his father castrate him for wickedness. Seems reasonable.

Nevertheless, the misogynist psychoanalyst condemning 51 percent of the population was able to prosper.

The Nazi regime burned his books and exiled him. But we have the Nazis to thank for a piece of Freud's black humor: "What progress we are making. In the Middle Ages they would have burnt me; nowadays they are content with burning my books." He made this horribly ironic quip in 1933. Concentration camps later murdered his four sisters.

A heavy smoker, Freud underwent over thirty operations for cancer.

His patient Princess Marie Bonaparte gave him a vase which later held his ashes. Another present from her was the couch that became the very symbol of psychoanalysis.

Freud received yearly nominations for the Nobel prize, but the committee finally shunned him for unscientific work.

Carl Jung (b. 1875)
The first (and second) thing to know is that, as a youngster, Jung thought he had two personalities. His alter ego was a prominent unnamed man, perhaps from the previous century.

After a concussion from a schoolyard casualty, Jung used the episode as an excuse to stay home from school. He managed to black out when he left for school or even when he did his homework, taking malingering to a new level. Even Ferris Bueller couldn't faint at will.

A fan of the supernatural, Jung frequented seances where he saw ghostly emanations. Here's a term he coined, not used today by the best people: *synchronicity*. *Synchronicity* apparently is a coincidence unexplained by natural phenomena. I call this New-Age nonsense. Just my opinion.

Individuation is "only experienced by those who have gone through the wearisome but indispensable business of coming to terms with the unconscious components of the personality." Namely psycho-analysis, and I bet wearisome is the word, and maybe even more so for the psychoanalyst, except that at least he's making his living from it.

All this weary work will finally tune the patient into the *collective unconscious*, and whatever that may mean, Jung's word for it, *Unbe-wusstes*, is more captivating. (I find it means innate "memories" of a past shared by all humans.) Jung added that "The Aryan unconscious has a greater potential than the Jewish unconscious. . . . The Jew, who is something of a nomad, has never yet created a cultural form of his own and as far as we can see never will." If he saw this as a fact, I'd say it lacked truth, not to mention tact, and especially in 1934.

During the war, as "Agent 488," Jung supplied the OSS with intel on Hitler's mental status.

His *Psychological Types* spurred the development of the Myers-Briggs Personality Type test which you yourself may have taken to show you what you already know. This is the test that hopes to outfox you by repeating the same question in different ways.

Last words: "Let's have a really good red wine tonight."

PHILOSOPHERS

Philosophers are always harping on the nature of knowledge. That's okay; after all, it is actually their job: *Philosophy* means "love of knowledge," and philosophers are in the business of *knowing*. It's not astonishing that their theories are full of the word "know."

Socrates (b. 470 BCE)
Plato described his teacher Socrates as ugly, snub-nosed, and with goggle-eyes, and luckily Socrates believed beauty was only skin-deep.

You've heard his hemlock history.

Motto: "Know thyself."

Plato (d. 347 BCE)
"I know that I know nothing."

For Plato, we human beings are clueless. Man ≈ a being raised in a cave who sees only imprecise shadows on the cave wall.

No offense to Plato, but I myself see reality perfectly well.

My father named our dog Plato. His children always assumed the name was Playdough. Take your pick.

Aristotle; *"The Philosopher"*; *"The Master"* (b. 384 BCE)
Some people describe him as the *last person to know everything there was to know* because 1) he had expertise in many areas, and 2) his was the last era where you *could* know everything. Happily, it's not my business here to debate the nature of "knowing" and "everything."

But Aristotle did garner other superlatives. A 2016 MIT study found Aristotle the most influential person ever. Other call him the smartest man ever and/or the first real scientist.

But not so fast. You could make a good case for his not knowing everything. For instance, some of his views remain controversial:

Although the moon is inexplicably without wings, stars are alive. Wind direction determines goat gender.

Eels don't procreate. Wrong! Freud's work on eel sex life (noted earlier) would show Aristotle a thing or two.

Jean-Jacques Rousseau (b. 1712)

We have the post-Impressionist painter Rousseau (Henri), who painted Primitive-School tigers and lions. But he's not *our* Rousseau.

The *philosophe* Jean-Jacques Rousseau was an artist in a different field: he wrote seven operas (influenced by the new genre *opera buffa*). Among Rousseau's contributions were *Les Muses Galantes* and *The Village Soothsayer*, which was used in an arrangement by Beethoven.

But more noteworthy is his other musical role. He invented a numerical notation method, explained in *Dissertation sur la Musique Moderne*. Example: *Twinkle, Twinkle Little Star*: |1 1 5 5 |6 6 5 -. (If this is beyond you, download the *Rousseau App*).

His familiarity with the stage may have prompted his conclusion that dramatic arts and sciences caused moral decadence. Artifice was not his cup of tea. This is the man who touted the "noble savage," man in a state of nature. "Man is born free but everywhere is in chains." But, he says, men have natural chains binding them together into a "general will" that should resist formal governmental fetters.

Immanuel Kant (1724–1804)

Portrait: Kant was short (five foot two inches) and hollow-chested. He had a crooked shoulder and a weirdly big head.

His health occupied him mightily. His view was that sleeping and longevity were inversely proportional: we should all sleep sparingly. Like Mark Twain, he suffered from constipation; sadly, Tesla's earthquake machine was a century away.

Kant's *Critique of Pure Reason* emphasized man's free will. I'm with him there. But as for *knowledge*, he believed our eyes *see* an object without knowing what it really is. I leave it to you to explore this abstract folderol.

Friedrich Nietzsche (b. 1844)

If nothing else, I've correctly and painstakingly spelled his name for your convenience.

When he was forty-five, Nietzsche witnessed a man beating a horse, whereupon he (Nietzsche) became mentally incompetent and paralyzed. Writer Alain de Botton says Nietzsche's reaction was to dance nude, to think he was Christ or the Buddha, and to plan to execute the Kaiser. His madness may have been due to late-stage syphilis. He (Nietzsche) died at age fifty-five.

Nietzsche's tenets were:

Perspectivism, which is apparently what it sounds like.

Herren- und Sklavenmoral, where the master-type wants dominance (which only the Jews know how to undermine) and the slave-type that wants the common good.

Nihilism: God is dead. Man is a zero. A loser. What the Nazis termed an Untermenschen, a low underling. He needs to become an *Übermensch* with new ideals.

In his *Also Spracht Zarathustra* Nietzsche depicts one such superior human being. His "Thus Spoke Zarathustra" (whom we know as Zoroaster) inspired Richard Strauss's music used in *2001: A Space Odyssey*.

Karl Marx; nickname: *Mohr*, "Moor" because of his
dark complexion (b. 1818)
Since Jews were officially banned from professional positions or public office, Marx's father had become a Lutheran, probably in order to practice law.

Alcohol and heavy smoking affected Marx's lungs, and his father suggested he plead ill health to dodge the draft.

Marx's radicalism limited his academic ambition, and the money his father sent him for tuition was spent on drinks. To avoid repaying loans, Marx used aliases such as "Monsieur Ramoz" in Paris, and "A. Williams" in London. His wife even pawned his pants. We can express his finances in terms of his politics: with his bank account constantly in the red, his mother suggested he earn some capital rather than just talking about it.

Indeed, red was his favorite color: In Paris he met Friedrich Engels, who had seen how his own family textile factory had abused the working class. Well-known historical facts don't belong here, so I won't explain how Marx used Hegelian dialectics to explain class struggles.

With Marx, Engels produced *The Communist Manifesto*. Engels also funded *Das Kapital*, which took Marx fifteen years to write, partly due to his health problems like hemorrhoids and boils, which were severe enough to prevent him from sitting.

Persona non grata in France and England, Marx thought he might move to Texas. He must have envisioned congenial authority-flouting Wild West outlaws.

His original London burial was in a special graveyard section for atheists. He would not be pleased that today it costs six dollars to visit his new grave. He is, however, commemorated by the Karl Marx Peak in the Tajikistan highlands.

Mohandas Karamchand Gandhi; Mahatma; "great-souled one"
(b. 1869)
Gandhi was a serious vegetarian who belonged to the London Vegetarian Society at a time when vegetarianism was weird.

He was another "father" to add to our list: As "Father of the Nation," he was more affectionately called "Bapu"—"papa" in Gujarati.

When advised to consume goat meat, he dreamed that a goat he'd eaten was whimpering inside him. That was the end of meat for Gandhi. But he did travel with a posse of she-goats. These were vetted by his secretary and milked on site lest some trickster give him cow's milk, which was known to arouse lust. Another trick to test his own sexual celibacy was sleeping nude next to teenage girls.

In common with Mark Twain, Kant, and Chairman Mao, Gandhi had chronic constipation, which is of no intrinsic interest except when the sufferer is a celebrity, and I hope I don't have to mention this problem again.

In South Africa, Gandhi declared Blacks were "troublesome, very dirty and live like animals."

ATHLETES

Amelia Earhart (b. 1897)

Where else do I put her? If not exactly athletic, hers was a physical feat. Unlike the Wright brothers, she's not quite a scientist.

Taxpayer expense: The search for Earhart cost US $4 million. Mind you, I don't object to this. I do consider the search justifiable, but that mission went a long way—to the remote Pacific islands—and that sum went a long way in 1937.

Earhart's first airborne adventure was to get into a wooden cube and rocket off a wooden box, ending with a crash landing. It was a roller-coaster that gave her the idea of a launch ramp, which her uncle helped her erect to extend the upward slant of a shed roof. The result was ripped clothing, facial bruises, and ecstasy at her failed "flight."

She learned plane-flying from one Neta Snook, who advised her in vain against buying her first biplane, the *Canary*. Speaking of unlovely names, though it's the fourth most popular name in the US this year, I'm sorry she was an *Amelia*, especially since her regrettable nickname was "Meelie."

Earhart founded *Amelia Fashions,* which seems a surprising enterprise for her until we learn some of its attire was made of parachute fabric and plane-wing material.

In 2014, her namesake Amelia Earhart (unrelated, unbelievably) of Colorado flew around the world with a co-pilot. Given her name, she felt bound to achieve this feat in honor of her predecessor. Today, her *Fly With Amelia* enterprise pays for flight lessons for teenaged girls.

Tom Brady (b. 1977)
Brady fell asleep in the locker room right before his very first Super Bowl game.

With a passion for Uggs boots, he gives each team member a pair for Christmas, whether they like them or not, and we can assume a high percentage of nots.

The exclusive TB12 diet: "high-protein, plant-based diet that excludes gluten, dairy, corn, soy, MSG, coffee, alcohol, GMOs, sugar, trans fats, overly processed foods, fruits, and nightshade vegetables."

Venus Ebony Starr Williams (b. 1980)
Note her beautiful name.

She personally designed a mattress for *GhostBed*. This is a "'performance mattress designed by athletes for athletes for better sleep recovery, promoting muscle and joint rejuvenation." What a racket, and I don't mean tennis.

Sports Illustrated showcased Venus when was only ten.

Her father coached her and Serena himself to keep them on a nonprofessional track while young. At the tennis academy, furthermore, the girls had encountered some racial bigotry.

Venus has won more than $40 million, second only to Serena in prize money.

Her serve reaches 129 miles per hour.

Serena Jameka Williams (b. 1981)
With Venus it's ghost beds. For Serena it's OPI nail polish—she has created various colors. At least (as far as I know) nail polish contains no ectoplasm.

Serena's hobby was making sewing patterns: she loved the technical specifications.

Her prize winnings amount to over $50 million.

Tiger Woods; Eldrick Tont Woods (b. 1975)
Middle name Tont, from his Thai mother. But his father called him Tiger—the nickname he had once given a friend in Vietnam.

Tiger cured his childhood stutter partly by nighttime conversations with his dog.

His mother likes him to wear the "power color" red at the end of a tournament.

He crashed his car (media rapture!) outside a resort he'd rented for $2 million.

After enjoying nonstop mistresses, he signed up for an inpatient sex rehab program.

O. J. Simpson (b. 1947)
If you know anything about him, it's that he was (curiously) not convicted of the murders of his ex-wife Nicole Brown Simpson and her friend Ron Goldman.

After the murder, the police discovered in his car a full set of false facial hair that O. J. had bought beforehand. He claimed it was to visit Disneyland incognito with his children.

During the media coverage of the police chase, a Domino's Pizza ad triggered a sales record for the pizza chain. Lucky timing.

What finally put O. J. in jail was his armed theft of sports collectibles, which he said he'd lost in a robbery.

WRITERS

Aeschylus (b. circa 525 BCE)
What's important to know about this Greek tragedian is his death. We know the facts from the Roman Valerius Maximus (*c.* 37 CE), who wrote about memorable historical events.

The hapless Aeschylus was hatless, and his bare head accounts for his demise. An eagle grasping a turtle was looking for a stone on which to smash open the shell of his prey. He took Aeschylus's bald head for a rock, where he dropped the reptile, which killed the blameless dramatist.

In Aeschylus, incidentally, we have another man for our paternity club: the Father of Tragedy, although I suppose you could dispute this in a good doctoral thesis.

Voltaire (b.1694 as *François-Marie Arouet*)
Voltaire found a flaw in the French lottery and used it to get (very) rich.

He was imprisoned once (in the Bastille) for poetry claiming the French ruler committed incest with his daughter and a second time for wanting to duel a member of the aristocracy.

Jane Austen (b. 1775)
Austen ran a mini-brewery. Her signature brew was molasses-flavored *spruce beer.*

Interest in beverages seemed to be a thing under the Austen roof. Legend has it that Jane's father's live-in student drank the servants' blood. Implausible, but where there's smoke there's fire.

The original name for *Pride and Prejudice* was "First Impressions." Not very perky, though it rams home the story's theme.

Oscar Wilde (b. 1854)

Best feature: *bon mots*—for example:

"My wallpaper and I are fighting a duel to the death. One or other of us has got to go."

"The only way to get rid of temptation is to yield to it."

"I never travel without my diary, one must always have something sensational to read on the train."

Homosexuality was a crime, and Wilde was very out. You could also say he was *out there*, as in painting dragons on his ceiling and covering the walls with peacock feathers.

He was sentenced to hard labor in prison, where he caught the meningitis that killed him. Graffiti on his grave (lipstick hearts and kisses) ended up irking the authorities; they finally surrounded the tomb with glass to prevent the tampering which I would call fitting tributes.

Agatha Christie (b. 1890)

Despite being impressively knock-kneed, she learned how to surf at Waikiki Beach, where she was photographed with her board in her 1922 bathing dress.

Christie hated birds and the odor of hot milk. *De gustibus non disputandum est*; remember Tesla's aversion to pearls and hair.

In 1926 she disappeared for eleven days. Nobody knows where she was. Neither did she; the days were blanketed in amnesia, she said. Her car was found crashed and empty. On a tip, her husband found her at Yorkshire inn, where Christie did not recognize him and where she'd checked in as "Teresa Neele." Her husband was having an affair with one Nancy Neele, which says something about Agatha Christie, though I don't know exactly what.

If you don't count the Bible or Shakespeare, Christie holds the all-time record for book sales (more than two billion books). Her play *The Mousetrap*, first staged in 1952, has had the longest run in dramatic history. When it was played at a prison—the nicely-named Wormwood Scrubs—a pair of prisoners took the opportunity to escape. Clearly even the guards were captivated by the plot.

During her volunteer stint as a World War I nurse, Christie noticed a careless pharmacist ("Mr. P") mistakenly preparing suppositories with an excess of a toxic drug. She "unintentionally" knocked the goods onto the shop floor and stepped on them. This same pharmacist also bragged that he carried a small quantity of curare around with him.

The publisher of *The Mysterious Affair at Styles* forced her to misspell *cocoa* (as coco), and readers let him know how they felt about this.

Quotations:

> "I married an archaeologist because the older I grow, the more he appreciates me."
> "Good advice is always certain to be ignored, but that's no reason not to give it."
> "Every murderer is probably somebody's old friend."

Christie says she spotted Hercule Poirot two times in the flesh—at the Savoy hotel and in the Canary Islands.

After she killed him off in one of her books, the *Times* wrote him a one-page obituary.

When Christie died, lights were lowered in London theatres.

Mark Twain; Samuel Clemens (b. 1835)
First and foremost, we've mentioned that Tesla helped cure him of a bout of constipation.

Steamboats, a main Twain motif, caused him plenty of grief. Nine times he almost drowned in the Mississippi River, though we might take this number with a grain of salt.

He was employed on the same boat where his brother died in an explosion.

Not astonishing, given Twain's humor, that as *nom de plume* choices, he considered Thomas Jefferson Snodgras; Epaminondas Adrastus Blab; also Sergeant Fathom, although he settled on another riverboat term.

One source states: "As a pilot, the term twain is used instead of two." And who minds the odd dangling modifier?

About human nature Twain was benignly cynical:

> "A classic—a book which people praise and don't read."
>
> "It is better to keep your mouth closed and let people think you are a fool than to open it and remove all doubt."
>
> "Anger is an acid that can do more harm to the vessel in which it is stored than to anything on which it is poured."
>
> "Do the right thing. It will gratify some people and astonish the rest."

"If man could be crossed with the cat, it would improve man, but it would deteriorate the cat."

When away from home, the ailurophile Twain rented a cat for a companion.

Twain says that exclamation marks are like laughing at your own jokes.

On its publication, *The Adventures of Huckleberry Finn* was banned by the Concord, Massachusetts library for its moral shabbiness and what we today call "language"—but not condemned for racism until the mid-1900s.

Twain earned $50,000 for his invention of a glue for scrapbook albums. His first patent, however, was for a clasp for "the vest, pantaloons, or other garment"—today a feature of bra straps. "It is obvious that my adjustable straps may be made non-elastic as well as elastic without departing from my invention; but I prefer to make them elastic. . . . The advantages of such an adjustable and detachable elastic strap are so obvious that they need no explanation."

But about patents he wrote (to Helen Keller): "It takes a thousand men to invent a telegraph, or a steam engine, or a phonograph, or a telephone or any other important thing, and the last man gets the credit and we forget the others . . . ninety-nine parts of all things that proceed from the intellect are plagiarisms, pure and simple."

Twain was a man who wore bright red socks with a white suit.

The background music in a video of Twain (filmed by Thomas Edison) is the *Dance of the Sugar Plum Fairy*—an aesthetically bold choice when "camp" wasn't yet invented.

Twain was born when Halley's Comet approached the sun most closely in its orbit, if "orbit" is correct comet behavior. His lifespan plan: "I came in with Halley's Comet in 1835. It is coming again next year, and I expect to go out with it. . . . The Almighty has said, no doubt: 'Now here are these two unaccountable freaks; they came in together, they must go out together.'" He did die a day after the comet's pass closest to the sun, a *parahelion*, the term of *cognoscenti* who do understand the orbital habits of comets.

The Brothers Grimm; Jacob and Wilhelm (b. 1785 and 1786)
First: Why do we say Brothers Grimm rather than Grimm Brothers? We don't say Brothers Wright or Brothers Everly.

Second, regardless of what we call them, their surname is dead on, and we shouldn't call them children's writers. They were philologists and lexicographers, although unfortunately Jacob died at the letter F. We know their names because they gathered German folk tales as part of their cultural studies: they didn't actually create *Cinderella, Snow White, Hansel and Gretel, Rapunzel, Little Red Riding Hood,* or *Rumpelstiltskin*. They did, however, write *Von dem Mäuschen, Vögelchen und der Bratwurst* (*The Mouse, the Bird, and the Sausage*).

Among the works that were later redacted was *How Some Children Played at Slaughtering*: Part II, Synopsis:

> One day, two brothers saw their father killing off a pig. They imitated what they saw and the older brother killed his younger brother. Their mother, who was giving the baby a bath, heard her child scream and abandoned the baby in the bath. When she saw what her eldest child had done, she took the knife out of her younger son's throat, and in her rage stabbed her older son in the heart. When the mother found out that meanwhile the baby had drowned in the tub, she felt an inconsolable desperation and committed suicide by hanging herself.

After a long day of work in the field, the father came home. Finding out that his whole family was dead, he soon also died from sadness.

Henry David Thoreau (b. 1817)

I'm not a fan. For one, look at him. The men of his era were stern, sour, sanctimonious, and a real turn-off with respect to hairstyle. (The women too.) And nowhere worse than in Boston, with intellectuals being the worst. In this cohort the mirth gene was a recessive gene, and since I use the word *cohort* you can take this as scientific fact.

My policy has always been to keep away from Transcendentalism, which moreover seems to involve Platonism and Kantian philosophy in *its* policy, and this book is not a reason to change it my position.

What can we say about Thoreau? I'm writing about oddities, and Thoreau defines dullness. Feel free to send me a very concise email explaining why you are a Thoreau buff and why I should be one too.

Thoreau's motto: "That government is best which governs least."

Bio highlight: he designed a pencil sharpener.

Another: Having very laudably caught a fish, he was grilling it in the sylvan setting that was his trademark. He started a forest fire that burned three hundred acres. Only his family's high standing kept him out of prison.

Victor Hugo (b. 1802)

To show off Hugo-style, cram a whole orange into your mouth. Chew and wash down with kirsch.

To force himself to write, he had his servants hide his clothes to prevent him from leaving the house.

The Vietnamese venerate Hugo as a saint.

When he lived on Guernsey, people collected the stones he had walked on.

In Paris, he lived on the Avenue Victor Hugo. He wanted his mail sent to "Mr Victor in his avenue, Paris."

Improbable but true: the town of Hugoton, Kansas was named for him.

A marker stands at the exact location of his conception.

At Hugo's death, Parisian brothels of Paris were shut for the day. Edmond de Goncourt says prostitutes wore black crepe over their genitalia.

Charles Dickens (b. 1812)
No question about his celebrity. A used toothpick of his was auctioned off in 2009 for 5,000 pounds.

A bookshelf in Dickens's house concealed a hidden door opening to a room containing a Batman costume.

As a child, Dickens wanted to marry Little Red Riding Hood. Good thing for Little Red Riding Hood that Dickens found another wife—she would have been better off wed to the wolf: Catherine Dickens told her neighbor, Edward Dutton Cook, that her husband had tried to commit her to an insane asylum. Cook reported, "He discovered at last that she had outgrown his liking. . . . She had lost many of her good looks." *Many*, but not *all*? Apparently, there was a look or two that remained, and Dickens should have treated her better.

Dickens belonged to the Ghost Club. Other members: Conan Doyle, of course, and Yeats. Less predictably, Charles Babbage, the mathematician who created the Difference Engine and father of the modern computer. The club looked into paranormal phenomena such as the Monster of Glamis Castle (the seat of the Thane of Glamis, namely MacBeth), and I say this is a monster that warrants further investigation.

The young Dickens had falling sickness, which we call epilepsy, and several of his characters evinced very accurate symptoms of the disorder.

He called his son Edward Bulwer Lytton Dickens in recognition of the author whose book began, "It was a dark and stormy night." Not everyone agrees with Dickens's high opinion. An "opening sentence to the worst of all possible novels" is the criterion for the winning entry of today's annual Bulwer-Lytton Fiction Contest

In Philadelphia you can see Dickens's pet raven, Grip, who was Poe's inspiration for *The Raven* and who underwent taxidermy.

Dickens liked his pets stuffed. The paw of his cat Bob forms the handle of a letter-opener.

He described Washington, DC as "the headquarters of tobacco-tinctured saliva . . . chewing and expectorating . . . [which] soon became most offensive and sickening."

Harriet Beecher Stowe (b. 1811)
Uncle Tom's Cabin (1852, banned in Southern states) helped earn her more money than any other ninteenth-century novelist.

Gustave Flaubert (b. 1821)
Flaubert won a government lawsuit over *Madame Bovary*'s depravity. Beyond that, there's nothing to say about his humdrum provincial life, reflected in the *Mœurs de province*—the novel's subtitle. Except that he was cosmopolitan enough to catch chronic syphilis in Beirut.

Leo Nikolayevich Tolstoy, Russian Толстой = "thick" or "fat" (b. 1828)
A deplorable nineteenth-century beard.

Tolstoy's philosophy of peaceful resistance influenced Martin Luther King and Gandhi.

He was well-known to the police and excommunicated by the Orthodox church. He invented a personal Christianity ("Tolstovstvo"), a sort of reform-centered anarchism.

He had to sell his house to pay his gambling debts.

Like Pythagoras, Hitler, and George Bernard Shaw (who said "animals are my friends . . . and I don't eat my friends"), Tolstoy was in the vegetarian vanguard.

When he was nominated for the Nobel prize, he removed himself from consideration.

Tolstoy hated Shakespeare. Maybe (Chekhov said) he was envious of Shakespeare's brilliance.

At age eighty-two, he changed into his peasant gear to escape into a rural setting away from society. Three weeks later he died.

Sir Arthur Conan Doyle (b. 1859)
I rate Sherlock Holmes as maybe the best literary character ever, though I'm happy to debate this assessment.

Conan Doyle staunchly believed in fairies. He spent (supposedly) "millions" of pounds touting them. He fell for some fake photos of fairies, which you can Google right now, noting that there were methods earlier than Photoshop for doctoring pictures.

I'm delighted to report that you can hear a recording, right now, of Conan Doyle after his death, speaking from the Other Side.

He asserted that he'd channeled Houdini's dead mother during a séance. Doyle's blunder was that he wrote down her words in English when the only language she knew was Hungarian. (Houdini's own mission, on the other hand, was to debunk spiritualism, and you'll know he was serious when you learn he wanted a legal ban on fortune-telling.)

Some allege that Conan Doyle invented Holmes's arch-foe Moriarty as someone to kill Holmes off at the Reichenbach Falls, so

Doyle could spend more time on spiritualism. He had to resuscitate him due to popular demand. Conan Doyle used the feeble pretext that Holmes had broken his fall via a fissure in the cliff-face. This lame plot device is what we call a *deus ex machina*: if a dramatist paints his protagonists into a corner, the theater techs use a machine to suspend a god-actor above the stage. Critics frown on this cop-out Act-V practice.

Under the *Cheaters* heading above, I mentioned the Piltdown Man hoax. Some attribute that con to Doyle—a trick to discredit scientists who had discredited one of his spiritualist compères.

Doyle, an MD, wrote that it was because he'd never attracted even one patient that he took up writing, and I for one am glad his medical career tanked. The closest he came to medicine was his narrator Dr. Watson, who misses all the elementary clues. Holmes should have assigned him *Detection for Dummies* as homework.

He was knighted for an essay in favor of the Boer War, for which his obesity kept him from enlisting.

Doyle was among the first car drivers in England.

George Bernard Shaw (b. 1856)
Shaw wrote Winston Churchill: "I am enclosing two tickets to the first night of my new play: bring a friend . . . if you have one."

Churchill answered: "Cannot possibly attend first night; will attend second, if there is one." Ouch followed by touché.

Other Shaw quips:

> "The play was a great success, but the audience was a dismal failure."
> "Those who cannot change their minds cannot change anything."

"Youth is wasted on the young."

"Dancing is a perpendicular expression of a horizontal desire."

He invented the *Shavian Alphabet*, a phonetic spelling involving >40 letters.

Shaw was so determined for it to succeed that he left money in his will to fund its creation.

He wrote much of his later work in a portable shack in his back yard.

Shaw won: a Nobel Prize, an Academy Award, and an Oscar. He died after falling from a ladder when he was pruning a tree.

Truman Capote; Truman Streckfus Persons (b.1924)
He took his stepfather's surname.

Capote's self-description: a "completely horizontal author." He could write only lying in bed or on a sofa. Ergonomically interesting.

His novella *Breakfast at Tiffany's* was made into a movie with a certain amount of ill will. Although Audrey Hepburn's role is iconic, Capote had envisioned Marilyn Monroe as he wrote it. He said that with Hepburn in the role, he wanted "to throw up." His original name for Holly Golightly was the ungainly "Connie Gustafson."

When he went out, he took his baby blanket along.

Capote spread the tale that the FBI's Hoover was a gay cross-dresser: Capote was out himself, and he loved to broadcast Hoover's stridently anti-gay hypocrisy.

Crazily superstitious, he avoided certain literary efforts on Fridays and refused to stay in any hotel room with any form of thirteen in its number.

Capote beat Humphrey Bogart in arm-wrestling.

J. K. Rowling; Joanne; pen name *Robert Galbraith* (b. 1965)
Rowling is pronounced "rolling."

For the writer so identified with Harry Potter, her pseudonym signaled a switch in genre. The Harry Potter movie rights netted her two billion dollars plus a percentage of the profits; Rowling wasn't worried about putting bread on the table. She wrote the "Galbraith" books for the fun of a new venture.

In *Little Women,* the character Jo March (Jo was Louisa May Alcott's alter ego) inspired Rowling as another "small, plain girl called Jo, who had a hot temper and a burning ambition to be a writer."

Rowling was ragingly famous, but she only once went incognito—she wanted to shop for a wedding dress "without any rubbish happening." She refused to discuss her disguise because she might want to re-use it.

She compares Quidditch to basketball, "which is probably the sport I enjoy watching most." Just like Kim Jong-un.

It tells us something about Rowling that, out of guilt over buying expensive jewelry, she donated the same price she had spent to a philanthropic outfit.

Rachel Carson, a.k.a. *"Saint Rachel"; "the nun of nature"* (b.1907)
To gain credibility, Carson initially used the non-gendered *nom de plume* "R. L. Carson." Although her views are too renowned for a book about unfamiliar facts, here are a few of her statements:

> "In this now universal contamination of the environment, chemicals are the sinister and little-recognized partners of radiation in changing the very nature of the world—the very nature of its life."

"Man is a part of nature, and his war against nature is inevitably a war against himself."

"Man undoes the built-in checks and balances by which nature holds the species within bounds."

At the time, DDT was considered so benign that the military sprinkled it on the skin against lice.

At age fifty-six, she talked about pesticides for a Senate subcommittee—in a wig to conceal the effects of chemotherapy. Except possibly to her girlfriend, Dorothy Freeman, she didn't reveal her terminal breast cancer and prior radical mastectomy lest her opponents claim her cause was personal.

E. B. White prompted Carson to publish her findings in *The New Yorker* articles that became her book *Silent Spring.*

Her words could be graphic. She described a squirrel poisoned by DDT: "The head and neck were outstretched, and the mouth often contained dirt, suggesting that the dying animal had been biting at the ground."

Her enemies fought poignancy with poignancy. The pesticide lobby claimed Carson would kill many young people in Africa. A character in a bestseller by Michael Crichton said, "banning DDT killed more people than Hitler." The site *rachelwaswrong.org* blames her for millions of malaria cases "because one person sounded a false alarm." Detractors labelled her a communist and a spy for a Russia that hoped to cripple American agriculture.

Ultimately, pesticide businesses agreed to end DDT production for the US market—provided Carson and her allies supported overseas sales.

Virginia Woolf (b. 1882)

Woolf's great-niece claimed she was anorexic; others posthumously diagnosed various other mental disorders. Starting in her mid-teens she underwent periods of major depression.

And it was not your normal garden-variety depression. One summer she went mad, believing that the birds were chirping in Greek and the bushes. Also present in the shrubbery was King Edward VII uttering blasphemies. She said only a woman with the hide of an elephant (which she lacked) could handle the suffering she was undergoing.

She tried suicide twice before succeeding the third time by walking into a river with her pockets full of rocks.

The young Woolf was a talented cricket player—unheard of for a girl. She had what was later called an "open marriage"; she had a love affair with Vita Sackville-West.

But for all her bohemian lifestyle, she had social biases. She once called Jews "disgusting" (never mind that she married one).

Vladimir Nabokov (b. 1899)

Nabokov wished there were a typographic symbol for a smile; he was the first to envision today's "smiley" face.

He said, "Sleep is the most moronic fraternity in the world . . . a mental torture I find debasing . . . I simply cannot get used to the nightly betrayal of reason, humanity, genius."

Nabokov had synesthesia—seeing letters and numerals in color. A variety of people enjoy this neurological quirk, including Billy Joel and Richard Feynman, who sees equations in color, things like Bessel functions in polychrome with "dark brown x's flying around."

Nabokov's mother's pearl necklace paid for some of his study at Cambridge.

Danielle Steel; Danielle Fernandes Dominique Schuelein-Steel (b. 1947)
Steel was elected an *Officier* of the French *Ordre des Arts et des Lettres*. Now I don't know about you, but I find it interesting that she has "significantly contributed to the enrichment of the French cultural inheritance."

Steel was raised largely in France.

Her second marriage took place in a prison cafeteria where she wed a bank robber.

Steel was the fourth best-selling American writer ever.

She writes her books on a 1946 typewriter.

Stephen King (b. 1947)
He's the same age as Steel. Unlike Steel and her typewriter, King prefers a Waterman-brand fountain pen to a computer.

He's made around $400,000,000 from his books.

King has been addicted to alcohol, Valium, and cocaine.

Just as Capote was dissatisfied with Audrey Hepburn in *Breakfast at Tiffany's*, King disliked Jack Nicholson as Jack Torrance in *The Shining*.

Ernest Hemingway (b. 1899)
Here's something that may give us an idea of the experiences Hemingway was working with: He had a sister close in age; for their first few years, their mother decided to treat them as girl twins. They both wore dainty dresses and had long hair. Truth is stranger than fiction.

One of Hemingway's diversions in Paris was carousing with James Joyce. Eventually he went to the Mayo Clinic for his hushed-up alcoholism. His many shock treatments—a notorious torture of that era—were useless.

He was on the FBI's radar, and I've mentioned this about a few of this book's personnel. J. Edgar Hoover had him shadowed.

Nicholas Reynolds, ex-CIA, who wrote histories about the armed services, claims that Hemingway was employed by both the OSS and the FBI—*and* further writes that he may have been a double agent in 1941 working for Stalin's NKVD, the earlier incarnation of the KGB.

Hemingway worked for hours standing at his desk, which was the top of a corner bookcase. His serious fans can buy (from furniture company Elm & Iron) the "Hemingway Bookcase," a piece of décor that "beguiles the senses."

One theory about his shotgun suicide is that his cumulative concussions amounted to traumatic brain injury. Another cites paranoia about his intelligence work across the Iron Curtain.

Ian Fleming (b. 1908)

Fleming suggested that President Kennedy tell Castro that nuclear missile testing caused impotence in bearded men.

Fleming did not lack real-world intelligence experience. During the war, he had cooked up *Operation Ruthless* to capture an Enigma machine; unfortunately, there was no enemy target available at the time.

He wrote at his vacation house in Jamaica, using a gold-plated typewriter. More formal than Hemingway's bookshelf.

He chose his character's name James Bond because it was the "dullest name" he'd ever heard. A "James Bond" was the author of a book Fleming owned—*Birds of the West Indies*, labeled by Wikipedia as the "definitive book on the subject," and maybe it wasn't only the ornithologist's name that was boring.

It was to the ambulance workers that he addressed his last words: "I am sorry to trouble you chaps."

POETS

William Shakespeare; "The Bard" (b. 1564)

"You have not experienced Shakespeare until you have read him in the original Klingon." So says an official in one of the Star Trek movies, of which there are inauspiciously thirteen. Being an "agglutinative language," Klingon is most likely a more lyrical choice than Shakespeare's cheesy English (Wikipedia).

Shakespeare wouldn't have written his sonnets if the plague hadn't closed theatres. Maybe if he'd had Zoom, he wouldn't have had to resort to poetry.

Among the terms English owes to Shakespeare: fashionable, eyeball, lackluster, wild goose chase, and one fell swoop.

Any actor will say you court disaster if you utter the name of the play "M—th." Call it "The Scottish Play." Superstition looms large in the theatre.

Blame Shakespeare for the American starling. In 1890, Shakespeare fan Eugene Schieffelin ("a mustachioed eccentric," according to *The New York Times*) wanted to introduce to the US every bird Shakespeare ever mentioned. Result: starlings fanned out from Central Park across the continent, and they're not as big a hit as *Henry IV*.

In 1613, sparks from cannon deployed onstage in *Henry VIII* ignited the thatch of the Globe Theatre's roof; within an hour the blaze had consumed the entire building. Luckily, some ale was on hand to douse one man's burning pants.

More recently (2016), archaeologists claimed to have found Shakespeare's bones in Stratford-upon-Avon. His head was missing, most likely because eighteenth-century thieves believed the skull would show them the physical source of a prodigious talent.

Whoever stole the skull risked trouble. Shakespeare's gravestone inscription was:

> Good friend, for Jesus' sake forbeare to dig the dust enclosed here. Bleste be the man that spares these stones, And curst be he that moves my bones.

Famous in his will: "'I gyve unto my wife my second best bed with the furniture," where "furniture" wasn't what we mean by the word; it was merely the furnishings of the bed, i.e., the bed linen. The bequest, written almost indecipherably between the lines of the document, looks like an afterthought.

I wouldn't have pegged Shakespeare as a devout Christian; maybe the beginning of his will is just customary boilerplate: "In the name of God Amen. I William Shakespeare . . . of Warwickshire gent., in perfect health & memory God be praised . . . first, I commend my Soul into the hands of God my Creator, hoping & assuredly believing through the only merits of Jesus Christ my Saviour to be made partaker of life everlasting. And my body to the earth whereof it is made."

To each Globe actor he left twenty-six shillings and eightpence (equivalent to £270 in 2021) to buy mourning rings.

John Donne (b. 1572)
Donne never got a university degree because he was a Catholic and refused to pledge allegiance to the Protestant Queen Elizabeth.

Due to parental disapproval, his marriage to Anne More was annulled, and both Donne and the officiant priest were jailed. Donne punned: "John Donne, Anne Donne, Un-done."

John Keats (b. 1795)

He was hardly more than five feet tall, and slender, which is the adjective every woman uses for herself in a personal ad, and male slimness too may have been in fashion in the nineteenth century. Someone posited that his dislike of dancing arose from his eyes being at the level of his partner's bosom.

When he got tuberculosis, he had to talk with his fiancée through a glass pane, an expedient we've recently experienced.

Emily Dickinson (b. 1830)

What I like about her better than her poems (which were very good, if you're okay with nouns capitalized at random, not to mention the dashes) is her taste in dogs: the best people prefer Newfoundlands. She said, "You ask of my companions. Hills—sir—and the sundown, and a dog as large as myself that my father bought me. They are better than human beings, because they know but do not tell."

What locals did know about her was her talent as a gardener. They didn't know she was a poet.

Of her nearly two thousand poems, only ten were published while she lived.

Dickinson loved music, or "moosic" as she pronounced it.

About this reclusive woman, I can believe the report that she sometimes talked to guests from behind the door of her bedroom.

Robert Frost (b. 1874)

He moved to England, where *A Boy's Will* was printed. American publishers had rejected his work. American publishers were wrong: Frost was the only poet to win the Pulitzer Prize four times.

His epitaph (the ending of one of his poems) reads, "I had a lover's quarrel with the world."

And now for something completely different, namely.

Allen Ginsburg (b. 1926)
Like Danielle Steel, Ginsberg was elected to a the French *Ordre des Arts et des Lettres* as a *Chevalier* (Ms. Steel, an *Officier*, outranked him).

The famous beginning of his poem "Howl": "I saw the best minds of my generation destroyed by madness." The poem was charged with obscenity, but the judge allowed its publication due to its "redeeming social importance."

He originated the term *flower power*.

Note that, according to Ginsberg, a reason for taking drugs was to hear again "the voice of God." His initial "voice" was that of poet William Blake, whom he at first assumed was God.

Here's some prescience from 1989:

> It looks like marijuana will slowly be legalized in the United States (since grandmother Margaret Mead came out for it the other day!). So I saw an AP dispatch yesterday that said that Governor Kirk of Florida called her "a dirty old lady."

Another comment on drugs:

> American Indians go after their vision-quest about the same time as Jewish boys get bar-mitzvahed. . . . So, I guess you could institutionalize or ritualize, ritualize the use of psychedelics as part of, like, a normal vision-quest for younger people, elective, you know, one of many. Maybe put the Boy Scouts in charge of that effort?

A *Washington Post* obituary calls him "an enthusiastic advocate of questionable pharmaceutical preparations."

He founded Jack Kerouac's School of Disembodied Poetics (in Tibet).

Ginsberg, who was gay, also belonged to the pro-pedophilia *North American Man/Boy Love Association*. The organization's goal was to decriminalize adult-child sex.

After abetting a theft, Ginsberg pleaded insanity. He avoided prison but was committed to a psychiatric institution.

An attendee at one of his readings asked whether he would ever really go literally "naked in the world," whereupon Ginsberg took all his clothes off.

Ginsberg and friends spent the night before his death having a sleepover.

T. S. Eliot (b. 1888)

An invitation from Virginia Woolf: "Come to lunch. Eliot will be there in a four-piece suit." But sometimes Eliot's formality seemed like part-façade. He was fond of whoopee cushions and exploding cigars. Once in London, he and his nephew purchased stink bombs from a local joke shop and set them off inside a hotel lobby.

A lot less appealing: Eliot was well-known for his anti-Semitic remarks.

Henry Wadsworth Longfellow (b. 1807)

His poetry gave us two useful expressions, so useful they're clichés: One is "ships that pass in the night." The second is "Into every life some rain must fall," immortalized in the Ink Spots' 1957 hit *Into Each Life Some Rain Must Fall*.

Longfellow once had Charles Dickens for Thanksgiving dinner.

His wife, Fanny, died while melting sealing wax, which ignited her dress. Longfellow, burnt as he tried to extinguish the fire, was unable to be at her funeral. From then on, his severe burns prevented him from shaving, hence his permanent beard.

Edgar Allen Poe (b. 1809)

At age twenty-seven he married his thirteen-year-old cousin.

He was an athlete: boxing, rowing, and above all swimming. He could swim seven miles against a river current.

When he was forty, he disappeared for a few days. He was in a state of delirium at an election hall; some say he had been "cooped"— drugged to coerce him to vote at multiple polling stations. We see this vanishing motif in authors (recollect Agatha Christie).

Poe's subsequent death, possibly due to rabies, remains an enigma.

Maya Angelou; Marguerite Ann Johnson (b. 1928)

Writing routine: Her office was a small hotel room.

After being raped by her mother's partner, Angelou spent five years without talking. She repeated this reaction during bad times throughout her life.

Angelou held interesting jobs. As a teenager she was a sex worker. After this she was a tram conductor. "I loved the uniforms." Later on, when the publisher of her serious work objected to her writing for Hallmark cards, she replied, "I want to be in people's hands . . . people who would never buy a book." She also wrote cookbooks.

Walt Whitman (b. 1819)

Again, with the beard. Not to mention the handlebar with an eight-inch wingspan.

Leaves of Grass: The "leaves" are his pages, which he compared to feeble and short-lived grass.

In the unexpected-fact department: Bram Stoker said he based his Dracula on Whitman's machismo.

Whitman so enjoyed being naked that he sometimes paid calls on his friends in the nude.

THE SUPER-RICH

The rich and famous pique everyone's curiosity. Here I'm going with not mere wealth but wealth with wackiness.

John D. Rockefeller (b. 1839)
His publicity people had him keep dimes on his person. He was supposed to hand a shiny new dime to every person he ran across.

Winston Churchill refused the Rockefellers' overtures about writing his biography; he rejected it for the insufficient $250,000 fee they proposed.

But the better stories are about his forebears and his descendants.

His father, "Devil Bill," assumed the role of a deaf-mute to sell snake-oil cure-alls. This same inventive man was also a fake otolaryngolist (known as Dr. William Levingston) and a bigamist with a secret second wife.

The autopsy of Nelson Rockefeller's son Michael found he drowned on a trip to New Guinea. Stubborn rumors, however, have him eaten by a crocodile, shark, or cannibals.

I've also mentioned the fabulist "Clark Rockefeller." It's hard to believe that the real Rockefellers weren't even aware (before his exposure) of his imposture because he plied his deceptive trade in high circles, and it's high-risk in any case to choose a pseudonym that invites questions. But my research says nothing about family reactions.

Cornelius Vanderbilt; "The Commodore" (b. 1794)
Repulsive muttonchops.

His writing was full of mistakes and phonetic spellings. A self-made man doesn't get a fancy education. He went from ferry cabin-boy to steamship and railroad tycoon.

Vanderbilt invented the ship's propeller.

Like Dickens, he sent his wife to a mental hospital, a convenient move that coincided with an affair with the governess.

J. P. Morgan (b. 1837)
Morganization = the practice of fixing insolvent enterprises.

His nose was pitted by rhinophyma, and if you care to know, that means "nodules, fissures, lobulations, and pedunculation." He avoided cameras, but he did say that the purple bulb center-face had become "part of the American business structure."

He lived in the first house to have domestic electricity installed.

Remember all those scientists whose deaths were honored by temporary business closings? At Morgan's death, the NYSE shut down for two hours.

John Éleuthère du Pont (b. 1938)
This chemicals magnate descended from gunpowder magnates.

He had a fake testicle inserted after an equestrian encounter with a fence.

Du Pont sold his Titanic ticket, having changed his voyage arrangements. Maybe he had seen the best of his life, though. Later on, he was imprisoned after murdering an employee. He marked the sentence by having all his buildings painted black.

Du Pont's contact with reality became increasingly thin. He sank cars in the pond where he also shot geese who were attacking him with witchcraft. Domestic X-ray devices protected the house from ghosts or invaders piercing the walls. Clocks "were sending him backwards in time." He toured his ranch in his personal M-113 armored personnel carrier. Poster child for paranoia.

Andrew Carnegie (b. 1835)
Carnegie's domain was steel. Noted for humility and philanthropy, he believed "the man who dies rich dies disgraced." His epitaph: "Here lies a man who knew how to enlist the service of better men than himself."

EXPLORERS

Marco Polo (b. 1254)

A native of Venice, Marco—with his father Niccolo and his uncle Maffeo—traded silks and spices; they were also commissioned by Kublai Kahn, ruler of the Mongol Empire, as envoys. Kahn even hired them to collect taxes from his territories, equipping them with a voucher (made of gold) for travel expenses.

Marco believed the rhinoceros he saw was a unicorn.

He provided Europe with a description of paper money, then unknown in the West.

A nineteenth-century zoologist named a longhorn-sheep species *Ovis ammon polii* in honor of Marco Polo's observations.

Christopher Columbus (b. 1451)

Columbus persuaded Ferdinand and Isabella they needed a route to Asia that would bypass the Muslim retail trade; he was astute enough to reckon sailing west would get him there. These royals later gave him the title "Admiral of the Ocean Sea." This sounds a little redundant, but it made sense. The Romans knew of two seas: the Mediterranean and the Atlantic. But the "Atlantic" took its name later. It started as the Sea of the god Oceanus. Later still, "ocean" became a common noun.

It was always a good idea to name your ship after a saint. Fifteenth-century sailors needed all the support they could get, and a patron saint was a good start. The *Niña* belonged to one Juan Niño, but her real name may have been the *Santa Clara*. The *Pinta*, whatever her official name, acquired the term for "painted lady," by which we mean prostitute. The *Santa Maria* was familiarly called *La Gallega*—the Galician, but in official records they didn't mess with the name *Santa Maria*—Queen of Heaven, Blessed Virgin, Mother of God, etc.

Religion permeated fifteenth-century Italian life. Discovering the fertile Orinoco River, Columbus supposed it was the Garden of Eden—a spot that would have been quite a find.

To keep his crew happy, Columbus kept them up to date with a fake, but optimistic ship's log.

He described the natives of Hispaniola ("little Spain") to the Spanish royals as ignorant of weaponry. They were healthy, naïve, timorous, and honest. All it would take was fifty of his men to enslave them. Columbus thanked the natives for their hospitality with the gifts of tuberculosis, influenza, and dysentery. Their unwitting revenge was to give them tobacco, where the fatalities came a little more slowly. Columbus, however, also brought them horses.

Amerigo Vespucci (b. 1451)
Lucky it was his first name that baptized a continent. His surname *Vespucci* means *evil wasps*.

Ferdinand Magellan; Fernão de Magalhães (b. 1480)
His name reminds us he was Portuguese. When Spain offered to underwrite his travel, the jealous king of Portugal dispatched agents to mess up Magellan's plans, ransack his home, and then kidnap him during his voyage.

After sailing west through his eponymous Straits, Magellan figured he'd reach China in several days—not four months.

Magellan was eventually killed in the Philippines by a tribe.

Henry Hudson (b. 1565)
His navigator Abacuk Pricket claimed Hudson appropriated extra food for himself. During the resulting mutiny the crew abandoned Hudson and eight others in a small boat in Hudson Bay, whence he disappeared for good. Useful tip: *Abacuk* means "he who embraces a wrestler."

Daniel Boone; "Big Turtle" (b. 1734)
He pioneered a route through the Cumberland Gap—a.k.a. the Wilderness Road to Kentucky, where he founded the outpost Boonesborough in Transylvania. Except we all know who really lived in Transylvania and it wasn't an American pioneer.

Shawnee chief Blackfish called him "Big Turtle" and took him in as a substitute for his dead son.

Edmund Hillary (b. 1919)
Altitude suited Hillary. He was six feet five inches tall.

He partially funded his expeditions by beekeeping.

Hillary claimed: "We have found rational explanations for most yeti phenomena."

He flew to the North Pole in 1985 with Neil Armstrong.

Neil Armstrong (b. 1930)
Armstrong could fly a plane before he could drive.

FASHION DESIGNERS

Gabrielle Bonheur "Coco" Chanel; Abwehr Agent F-7124 (b. 1883)
Before leaving her home (the Ritz) each morning, Chanel called her salon to alert them to spritz it with Chanel No. 5.

Marilyn Monroe used this perfume at night. She said she went to bed wearing "just a few drops of Chanel No 5."

Chanel spied on her salon shows to judge how the attendees responded to her latest fashions. We have her to thank for the "little black dress"—a fashion standard ever since.

Another icon is the Chanel Purse, a quilted shoulder bag. A used Chanel bag will run you $4975. "Very Good" condition, "a slight odor in interior. Moderate wear on exterior corners, scuffs and marks underneath flap, wear and minor bubbling on strap. Wear in interior, scratches on hardware, light odor in interior. Moderate wear on exterior corners, scuffs and marks underneath flap, wear and minor bubbling on strap. Wear in interior, scratches on hardware." A steal, depending on whether you mean buyer or seller.

Some believe it was Chanel who made suntans chic.

One opinion of another designer: "Saint Laurent has excellent taste. The more he copies me the better taste he displays." She should know. As she says, "I don't do fashion. I am fashion." At the Ritz she lived cheek-by-jowl with Nazi officers. Accused of collaboration, she prudently moved to Switzerland.

Coco had flings with Picasso, Stravinsky, and the Duke of Westminster.

About death, she said: "I would like to leave if I had the wish to go to Heaven and dress the angels." She wore her favorite Chanel suit in her coffin.

Guccio Gucci (b. 1881)
As an elevator boy at the London Savoy Hotel, Gucci eyed the clothes of the likes of Marilyn Monroe, who once said, "Give a girl the right shoes, and she can conquer the world."

He started his career designing high-end equestrian leather saddle bags: his brand logo is a horse's bit.

Christian Dior; "Tyrant of Hemlines" (b. 1905)
Dior depended heavily on psychics.

A few quirks marked his fashion shows. Models held white lilies. One outfit in every show was called "Granville" after his local city.

He spent hours in a green marble tub complete with swan-shaped taps.

A budding anarchist at university, Dior looked into communism in the USSR.

Some allege he died from choking on a fishbone.

Yves Saint Laurent (b. 1936)
Schoolmates bullied him for his effeminacy. Less than three weeks after joining the army, he had a mental meltdown and went through shock treatments, which were no fun in those days.

> "It pains me physically to see a woman victimized,
> rendered pathetic by fashion."

Chinese Americans protested his *Opium* perfume, which in some countries was banned for a name glorifying the drug. I call this sanctimonious, although maybe one ad went too far, showing a woman rubbing the vein in her arm and then hallucinating.

Calvin Klein (b. 1942)
Brooke Shields's ad ("Nothing comes between me and my Calvins") shocked people who couldn't stand the thought of going without underwear.

I can personally attest that his signature blue jeans made even a second-rate body look pretty good.

A co-worker of mine wore Calvin Klein's *Eternity* perfume, advertised as "fruity-floral. Its "top notes" are Pear, Blackcurrant, Bergamot. Heart Notes: Peony, Rose Absolute, Jasmine Absolute. Base notes: Patchouli Coeur, Sensual Skin Musk, Amber. Fact: it smells like pesticide.

Gianni Versace (b. 1946)
Towards the end of his life Versace didn't go out much: an inoperable ear tumor had disfigured his face.

ARTISTS

Sandro Botticelli; Alessandro di Mariano di Vanni Filipepi (b. 1445)
Why was Sandro Filipepi, which I call a jaunty little surname, called Botticelli?

He was raised by his thickset older brother nicknamed *botticello,* "barrel," for his stout physique.

Since everyone painted the Madonna and Child, painters liked to add a gimmick, among them *Botticelli's Madonna and Child with a Pomegranate*; his Madonna *of the Book, of the Sea,* and *in an Alcove with Roses Behind.* Flowers were popular; other painters' works include Madonna *of the Pinks* and *of the Carnation,* not to be confused with Leonardo's *Madonna of the INcarnation.* And let's not forget other artists' *Madonna of the Spindles, Madonna of the Harpies, Madonna with a Long Neck,* and *Madonna of the Stairs.*

By the way, don't assume all Madonnas are in dusty Italian churches. A dozen copies of *The Madonna of the Trail* (statue) embellish the National Old Trails Road (the Ocean-to-Ocean Highway). Placed by the Daughters of the American Revolution, the statues honor frontier females.

But this entry was meant to belong to Botticelli; we're far afield.

He was one of the artists who painted small panels of the Sistine Chapel. But besides Christian themes in art, Botticelli's painted classical subjects. Of *The Birth of Venus*, a PBS special said: "Designed to be hung above the marital bed, it was a daring celebration of human desire. The painting was so controversial it was kept behind closed doors for half a century."

Botticelli is rumored to have set fire to his "pagan" paintings at the command of Savonarola during the bonfire of the vanities.

Leonardo da Vinci (b. 1452)
In his twenties, Leonardo was accused of sodomy—a capital crime. He was acquitted, but for his reputation's sake, he lay low in Milan until the scandal blew over.

If you care to credit such things, a software program analyzed Leonardo's Mona Lisa as 83 percent happy, 9 percent disgusted, 6 percent fearful, and 2 percent angry.

Leonardo DiCaprio was named after him.

Michelangelo Buonarroti (b. 1475)
Michelangelo's clothes were (apparently) so filthy they adhered to his body; when he died, they had to be removed like a skin, a scene I'd rather not dwell on.

Edgar Degas (b. 1834)
The painter Pissarro called Degas a "ferocious anti-Semite."

Degas's colleagues elaborate on his character. According to Renoir, "All his friends had to leave him; I was one of the last to go, but even I couldn't stay till the end." Manet claimed he was incapable "of loving a woman."

Behind the gauzy ballerinas was a grotesque brute.

Auguste Renoir (b. 1841)
When arthritis crippled him, Renoir bound his hands in cloths and fastened his brush to them. While painting, he cradled a cat in his lap to warm himself: the Institut Pasteur verified his paintings from their traces of cat fur.

Charles Gounod fostered the boy Renoir's singing talent and got him into a paying choral group, but the youth instead got a job painting porcelain.

Degas was not the only antisemitic artist of the period. Manet's niece cites Renoir: "[Jews] come to France to earn money, but if there is any fighting to be done they hide behind a tree." He took the same stance during the Dreyfus affair.

Claude Monet (b. 1840)

His *Impression, Sunrise* triggered the term *Impressionism*.

He diverted some of a nearby river to make his water-lily pond, which he spanned with a small Japanese bridge. He hired a man to dust the flowers daily. The locals claimed the invasive species he introduced—plants from Egypt and South America—were toxic.

Cataract surgery caused him to register a color—like ultraviolet—unseen by most of us. Following the surgery, he demolished up to five hundred pictures he had painted in the time before his vision had been improved.

As a penurious young man, Monet attempted suicide. Luckily his leap off a Paris bridge didn't work.

Paul Gauguin (b. 1848)

Exotica comes to mind.

But his career didn't begin with the Polynesian women and icons. He was a stockbroker at the Paris Bourse with what would now be a six-figure salary.

Nor did Gauguin go native in a mood of tropical euphoria. He painted the Crucifixion with his own face to portray his personal solitude and anguish. His colossal *Where do we come from? What Are We? Where Are We Going?* are existential questions not springing from a mellow state of mind. Human mortality consumed his thoughts.

Gauguin used opioids and alcohol to treat syphilis and a leg sore. He died from an overdose of morphine on Atuona, Hiva Oa, Polynesia; his doctor and his brother attributed his death to suicide.

Dental addendum: his teeth were discovered in a Polynesian well. The cavities suggested he'd eaten a Western diet, and when DNA analysis compared the teeth with his grandson's DNA, scientists found it 90–99 percent likely they were Gauguin's. Non-dental items in the well, such as a paint-covered coconut-rind paintbrush, seem to prove the teeth are his.

Henri Matisse (b. 1869)
It never occurred to him to paint until, at age twenty, he was convalescing from appendicitis.

Grant Wood (b. 1891)
This is supposed to be a book about famous people. But this artist's name is less well-known than his painting *American Gothic*.

The title of the picture refers to the style of the house behind the farm couple: it's Carpenter Gothic, which you can easily distinguish from, say, fifteenth-century Flamboyant Gothic. It is in fact the Dibble house in Eldon, Iowa—now a State Historic Site. You can visit it, and they have a pitchfork and costumes available *gratis* so you can recreate and customize the scene.

In the original, it was Wood's sister and his dentist who posed for him. A few embittered residents viewed the picture as a mockery of the flyover states.

Pablo Diego José Francisco de Paula Juan Nepomuceno María de los Remedios Cipriano de la Santísima Trinidad Martyr Patricio Clito Ruíz y Picasso (b. 1881)

As a diminutive newborn, he was deemed stillborn until an uncle spotted movement and sent a cloud of cigar smoke at him to liven him up. His name made up for his small size.

In his early teens, Picasso was introduced to prostitutes by his father so as to give him sexual experience. He became a noted ladies' man. But his girlfriends had to measure less than his own height of five feet four inches.

One practice of his was firing blanks from a pistol he kept handy. His targets were people who bored him or who spoke ill of Cézanne.

He held two records: the most works by one artist and, at the time of his death, the wealthiest artist ever.

A third (somewhat flattering) record: of all painters' works, Picasso's were most frequently stolen.

MUSICIANS

Note: I'm going to leave out most of our contemporary popular musicians on the grounds that concerning their stories, *People* magazine has already scooped me. I'll make an exception, however, for two royals, each of them nobler than any crummy monarch, certainly outranking mere aristocrats like "Duke" Ellington or "Count" Basie or "Lady" Gaga. Not even Prince Rogers Nelson (better known as "Prince" *tout court*) ever wore a royal crown. The following two individuals are a *bona fide* king and a *bona fide* queen.

Elvis "The Pelvis" Presley; "The King" (b. 1935)
Elvis had a stillborn identical twin. Can you imagine a second Elvis?

During many of his shows, he didn't play his own guitar. TV emcee Milton Berle told him: "Let 'em see you, son"; and Elvis flaunted his pelvis as though he were rehearsing for his future "Blue Hawaii" days in hula country.

A Floridian magistrate labelled Elvis "a savage" for "undermining the youth."

One newspaper review claimed, "Elvis' singing wasn't sexy, it was pornographic." Another journalist's graphic words: "As he stands up there clutching his guitar, he shakes and shivers like he is suffering from itchy underwear and hot shoes."

With Steve Allen threatening to cancel Presley's upcoming performance on his show in July, Elvis was pressured into toning down his movements. On July 1, 1956, Steve Allen introduced "the new Elvis Presley" as Elvis walked onstage in a tuxedo and tails to set things right with the older generation. Allen declared this less threatening appearance Presley's "first comeback."

To add fuel to the fire, one month later a judge in Jacksonville, Florida threatened Presley with jail time if he did not restrain himself during his live concerts there on August 10-11, 1956. Elvis was reduced to moving only his pinky finger to keep the peace. This change in performance style is what led up to Presley's highly anticipated appearances on *The Ed Sullivan Show*.

Since Presley had already toned down his act for *The Steve Allen Show*, it seemed that Ed Sullivan would not have to worry about Elvis causing any controversy. But surprisingly, Ed Sullivan still felt the need to censor Elvis.

If you're an idol, appearance matters. Elvis started blackening his hair with shoe polish until he switched to Miss Clairol 51 D ("Black Velvet)." He dyed his eyelashes too.

Instead of a dog or cat he owned Scatter, a chimpanzee.

Elvis was mysophobic—terrified of germs (check the pronunciation so you can use it yourself). Sometimes his concern over health was healthy. He helped public health authorities fight their polio effort by staging his own public vaccination.

That's not to say that Elvis was personally healthy. Consider the Elvis Sandwich, as revolting a meal as ever hit a stomach. The recipe: two slices of bread crammed full of peanut butter, jelly, a banana, and a few slices of bacon.

Next to his diet, his penchant for guns was downright benign— they were just for play. He reportedly shot at a television and once sent a bullet into the headboard of a sleeping girlfriend to "grab her attention."

Eventually he was wrangling prescriptions from multiple doctors simultaneously.

But his drug schemes got more ambitious; he got President Nixon to hire him as a narcotics inspection agent. (Disguised as a badged policeman, he'd stop drivers so he could treat them to an autograph.)

Elvis wore his hair in the "pompadour" style, which at the time was known as a quiff, a jelly roll, or a ducktail, commonly called a "duck's ass" (or DA)—dubbed by *GQ* "one of the greatest cuts in grooming history." As hair gel, he used, appropriately, the brand Royal Crown. His hairdresser saved locks of his hair and sold them at auction after his death. In 2002, one strand went for $115,000.

Aretha Franklin; "The Queen of Soul" (b. 1942)
Another regal figure. If Elvis was the king, Franklin was the queen.

She had a baby at the age of twelve.

Michigan's Department of Natural Resources named her voice a "natural resource of the state."

Compared to Elvis, her relationship with Nixon was poor. The president called her a "dangerous terrorist."

The FBI monitored her closely, their standard M. O. with artists, as noted above.

One of Aretha's performance contracts stipulated, "I need that air conditioning off." When, during a rehearsal, she discovered it was turned on, she walked out.

She told *Vanity Fair* that her greatest mistake was not knowing how to read music.

CLASSICAL COMPOSERS

Pyotr Ilyich Tchaikovsky (b. 1840)

One source call him "a sensitive individual," where the word "understatement" comes to mind when we learn about the stage fright. Tchaikovsky conducted one-handed: with his other hand he gripped his chin to keep his head from flying off. I'm not making this up.

Tchaikovsky started his career as a practicing lawyer.

He hated his *1812 Overture* honoring the battle of Borodino against Napoleon.

It had been his own notion to use actual cannons, but he thought it turned out too "noisy."

Officially, he died of cholera from drinking unboiled water. But some historians claim cholera even in a corpse would have been too infectious to allow his open-casket funeral. An alternative theory is suicide after he was outed as gay.

Ludwig van Beethoven (b. 1770)

At eight-year-old Beethoven's concerts, his father lied about his age, hyping the prodigy by announcing that he was only six.

Beethoven was deaf by the time he was given a fancy piano, which he couldn't hear. But with his perfect pitch he didn't need his working physical ears. Another of his techniques for composition was plunging his head into chilly water. He said, "Music is like a dream. One that I cannot hear."

A few other comments:

"Music is the one incorporeal entrance into the higher world of knowledge which comprehends mankind, but which mankind cannot comprehend."
"Music should strike fire from the heart of man and bring tears from the eyes of woman."
"To play a wrong note is insignificant. To play without passion is inexcusable!"
"The guitar is a miniature orchestra in itself."

In his era, cheap wines contained lead to improve taste. The lead didn't help Beethoven's failing liver. He died during a thunderstorm, which maybe reminded him of his Pastoral Symphony's movement "The Thunderstorm." In any case, his sense of humor remained intact; when physicians emptied him of twenty-five pounds of abdominal fluid, Beethoven compared the doctor to "Moses, striking water from a rock."

Chuck Berry said, "Roll Over Beethoven. Tell Tchaikovsky the news." (Depending on your age, you may not know who Chuck Berry was. A poll of six of my children found that while the older ones had heard of Berry, the youngest two (born in the 1990s) had not.

Johann Sebastian Bach (b. 1685)
A charlatan performed cataract surgery on Bach, blinding him and causing his death, within four months, from intractable glaucoma because of pupillary block, or secondary to phacoanaphylactic endophthalmitis (Finnish researcher Ahti Tarkkanen). Undergoing the same operation a century and a half later, Monet would get off light (literally): afterwards he could see normally invisible colors of the spectrum.

Antonio Vivaldi; "The Red Priest" (b. 1678)
The asthma which cut down on his parish responsibilities permitted him to turn his attention to composing.

Richard Wagner (b. 1813)
Well-known as a German nationalist and anti-Semite, Wagner wrote a poorly received article, *Jewishness in Music.*
He had a penchant for rich fabrics and expensive fragrances.
His operatic epic *Der Ring des Nibelungen* originates in the Germanic myth of a race of dwarfs.
When in debt (often) Wagner simply left Germany.

Wolfgang Amadeus Mozart; Johannes Chrysostomus Wolfgangus Theophilus Mozart (b. 1756)
Named in his honor, *Eleutherodactylus Amadeus* is a frog species in Haiti with an unusually wide range of musical vocalizations.
The *Rolling Requiem* project: on an anniversary of 9/11, at 8:46 a.m. in local time zones worldwide, choral groups sang Mozart's *Requiem Mass in D Minor.*
Today, some scholars claim Mozart had Tourette's syndrome, citing his odd tics and extreme fidgeting, not to mention his often-inappropriate behavior, as if his motto was *épater les bourgeois.* Consider the lyrics of his *Canon in B-flat major*—"Leck mich im Arsch" ("lick my ass"). He gleefully flaunted his unorthodoxy. Example: performing in a shocking-red coat and gold-colored tricorn hat.
And he was a disorganized slob. Luckily the musicologist Köchel catalogued his works.
Mozart's credo (in a letter to his father): Music must be simple enough for a coach driver to sing.

He wrote to his wife, Constanze, that in his heart was nothing but ice.

He may have died of trichinosis (pork not cooked enough to kill the roundworms). Or maybe, based on analysis of his (purported) skull, of brain hematoma.

VARIOUS RELIGIOUS TYPES

Saint Ambrose (b. 397)

He's credited with introducing silent reading to the Romans. Evidently it hadn't really occurred to them that they could read to themselves rather than *viva voce*; silent mode was not only (obviously) unheard but also unheard-of. Augustine described this wacky extraordinary novel practice: "When Ambrose read, his eyes ran over the columns of writing and his heart searched out the meaning, but his voice and his tongue were at rest." *Mirabile dictu*! (or rather, *non dictu*).

مَحَّ أبن بَبَع اللّهِ, *Muhammad ibn 'Abd Allāh* (b. circa 570)

The Prophet worked as a goatherd on the trade convoys to Damascus.

In his literal man-cave at Hira, the Angel Jibreel Gabriel visited him and told him to read up on Allah. Unfortunately, the embarrassed Muhammad hadn't learned to read.

He married nine-year-old Sayyida Aicha.

Muhammad was known for his integrity; his cognomen was "The Trustworthy."

He endorsed Moses's commandment nixing graven images and warned his followers against idolatry, especially in the form of representations of himself. He never preached that he was divine.

Muhammad taught four principles about dining: halal food, sharing mealtimes with others, and beginning and ending the meal with God's name.

Extended praying made his legs swell.

Joan of Arc; "The Maid of Orléans"; "La Pucelle" (b. circa 1412)
Joan was born *Jehanne Tarc.*

When she wore boys' clothes before the king, she was accused of both heresy and cross-dressing.

Her riposte to a priest's question about the language of the voices she heard: "better French than you speak."

Some modern doctors attribute her visions to schizophrenia or, of course, bovine tuberculosis.

Because she fought England, French right-wingers today use Joan as an anti-immigration symbol.

The fashion-forward reader will already know that in 1909 the Parisian hairdresser Monsieur Antoine modelled a bob hairdo after Joan of Arc.

After a few moments at the stake, her body was briefly withdrawn to prove she was a mere human and susceptible to burning.

Martin Luther (b. 1483)
In his early twenties, during a violent thunderstorm, Luther vowed that if he escaped with his life, he'd enter the Black Cloister as a monk. Being a cloistered brother did not keep him from being a bit of a frat brother. Not exactly a party animal, but he believed, "Sometimes we must drink more, sport, recreate ourselves, aye, and even sin a little to spite the devil." His metaphor: sins were the excreta of the devil.

When the Catholic Church hunted Luther down, Prince Frederick the Wise rescued him and Luther went on the lam as "Junker Jörg."

He claimed that since Christ was murdered by Jews, they should be persecuted.

Joseph Smith, Founder, Church of Jesus Christ of Latter-day Saints
(b. 1805)

When Joseph was fourteen, a would-be murderer asked around about where he could find him. A helpful friend of Joseph's informed the killer, "He went to heaven on Hyrum's white horse and we are fixing this kite to send his dinner to him." The ill-intentioned gunman fired a shot and fled—unseen by anyone else.

On another occasion a bullet missed Smith but hit a cow.

Like Andrew Jackson and Tchaikovsky, he was plagued with stage fright. His legs "trembled like Belshazzar's" (as you no doubt know, the latter was the biblical king who was terrified by "the writing on the wall").

The angel Moroni—Smith claimed, although in hindsight, perhaps it was the angel *moron*—directed him to unearth some gold plates revealing Jewish and Christian traditions of a pre-Columbian people.

Moroni told him the location of these plates but made him visit the spot annually: not until the fourth year did he manage to dig them up. Buried with the plates was a special pair of spectacles to help translate the plates from the reformed Egyptian language. The lenses, named Urim and Thummim, consisted of a pair of "clear rocks," and who am I to call that phrase an oxymoron? A pity that they were incomprehensible. Not that it would matter since no one except eleven "witnesses" ever saw them.

By 1830, Smith and others had translated these records into his *Book of Mormon,* Mormon being the prophet to whom Jesus had originally given the plates.

Smith returned them to their cave in the Hill Cumorah off Route 90, where you will find the Visitor's Center providing both a trail to the Angel Moroni Monument and a "live virtual tour," ditto on the oxymorons.

When people hunted for these artifacts, which were like a Mormon Holy Grail, Smith had to bury them in a bin of beans.

The *Word of Wisdom* was updated in 2016 to ban vaping. Included was a further beverage alert:

> The word coffee isn't always in the name of coffee drinks. So, before you try what you think is just some new milkshake flavor, here are a couple of rules of thumb: (1) If you're in a coffee shop (or any other shop that's well-known for its coffee), the drink you're ordering probably has coffee in it, so either never buy drinks at coffee shops or always ask if there's coffee in it. (2) Drinks with names that include café or caffé, mocha, latte, espresso, or anything ending in -ccino usually have coffee in them and are against the *Word of Wisdom.*
> Green tea and black tea . . . are both against the *Word of Wisdom* . . . Also, iced tea is still tea.

Possibly Smith had had up to forty spouses, which included minors and married women. (He ordered his acolytes to annihilate the periodical that published this datum.)

Smith and his saints were heavily harassed. When he was being tarred and feathered, his assailants chipped one of his teeth when trying to force tar into his mouth. From then on, his speech had a faint sibilance. He spent a lot of time eluding enemies, where one ploy was wearing a dress.

It was more than harassment, in fact. A bounty of a thousand dollars was posted for his head. Ultimately his adversaries paid an alcohol-incited rabble to assassinate him (resulting in some people converting to Mormonism out of sympathy). At Smith's funeral, additional fake decoy-caskets prevented sabotage.

Brigham Young (b. 1801)
Bad beard (as we've noted, a staple of the nineteenth century).

When Brigham Young spoke in tongues, Joseph Smith recognized the lingo as "Adamic language." Even without his magic translation aids.

Young defended slavery: "This colored race have been subjected to severe curses . . . which they have brought upon themselves." And he meant it: "If the white man who belongs to the chosen seed mixes his blood with the seed of Cain, the penalty, under the law of God, is death on the spot."

The Hosanna Shout: Wave a white handkerchief and say "Hosanna, Hosanna, Hosanna to God and the Lamb" three times; end with "Amen, Amen, and Amen."

With fifty-six wives and fifty-seven children, Brigham Young trumped Joseph Smith.

Martin Luther King Jr.; Michael King (b. 1929)
When he was five, his father gave him the name we know him by.

King says a white childhood friend who shunned him triggered his anti-racist work.

Martin Luther King Jr. and George Washington are the only Americans honored by a national holiday.

L. Ron Hubbard (b. 1911)
Founder of the *Church of Scientology* (1950), Hubbard was interested in the occult even before he started his church. To invoke the Goddess Babalon, he performed a sex magic rite with a founder of the Caltech Jet Propulsion Laboratory, Jack Parsons. The team effort

called for Parsons to enjoy sexual pleasure while Hubbard kept an eye on the astral plane.

After reacting to a dental anesthetic, Hubbard wrote his manuscript *Excalibur*, which contained the germ (and I use the term advisedly) of his *Dianetics* theory. Hubbard's *caveat* to readers: "four of the first fifteen people who read it went insane." He told President Kennedy that Russia was willing to pay him $100K for the manuscript.

The *Dianetics* system uses mental *engrams*—bad events you've experienced. Luckily, you can be *audited* to work backwards through them until they are innocuous, and your status is *Clear*. Your auditor detects your "spiritual state or change of state" with an *Electropsychometer (E-Meter)*, "a religious artifact that helps the auditor and you, the preclear, locate areas of spiritual distress or travail." See how you yourself would do in a few sample audit questions:

> "Have you ever had unkind thoughts about L. Ron Hubbard?"
> "[In a former life] Have you ever destroyed a culture?"
> "Did you come to Earth for evil purposes?"
> "Have you ever zapped anyone?"

Dianetics is clearly a sound practice, but unaccountably both the *Journal of the American Medical Association* and the *American Journal of Psychiatry* rejected a paper on this therapy method.

Federal officials (the FBI and Interpol) started to notice Hubbard. The IRS ended the tax break it had given his religious institution, since Hubbard used his non-profit for personal gain. And the FDA didn't like his "radiation cures."

In a US Navy report on Lieutenant (junior grade) Hubbard: "This officer . . . is garrulous and tries to give impressions of his importance. He also seems to think he has unusual ability in most lines."

Hubbard wasn't a hit with the Navy, but he did like the ocean. Take, for instance, the *Sea Org*, a practice where Scientology's executive committee went to sea in a kind of marine monastery. These individuals alone are authorized auditors. Today's *Freewinds* is a cruise ship aboard which "lives are transformed." The *Advanced Organization* teaches auditors about the material universe, the Eighth Dynamic, and "how to play and win the game of life."

David Miscavige, Captain of the *Sea Org* (b.1960)
Not as familiar a name as Hubbard, but worth a few paragraphs.

He claims that he had a headache while working on a pyramid scheme (named "Holiday Magic"). He was cured by his collaborator, who was luckily a Scientologist and advised him to pass his headache to his reflection.

Miscavige was a born manager: He instructed his underlings to spit on an underperforming employee.

Another type of corrective action, which he might or might not have run by HR, was The Hole, a training module where unsatisfactory performers received career coaching with thrashings or water torture. Or even musical chairs where losers were transferred to outlying offices, perhaps in the taiga or the Tibetan Plateau, without their families.

Miscavige's father described his son with an analogy:

David the child: David the Scientologist :: Dr. Jekyll: Mr. Hyde.

SELECTED SAINTS

Not just saints but also various persons of that nature, namely super-nature.

Moses (b. fourteenth-thirteenth century BCE)
Of all people, Moses should have been an eloquent speaker. But no. "I am slow of speech," he said to God. He felt unqualified to speak: "I am of uncircumcised lips, and how shall Pharaoh hearken unto me?" where uncircumcised means not pure. His brother Aaron did some of his public speaking for him.

King Solomon (tenth century BCE)
Researchers argue about whether he was real, or how real. The reliability of Biblical accounts seems to depend on the date of the union of Israel and Judah, and that's enough geopolitics for us.

From the Book of *Chronicles*: "Once every three years the ships of Tarshish used to come bringing gold, silver, ivory, apes, and peacocks." Archaeology supports Solomon's fabled wealth; nearby mines produced precious metals.

From the Book of *Kings* about Solomon's Temple in Jerusalem: "Solomon overlaid the house within with pure gold: and he made a partition by the chains of gold before the oracle; and he overlaid it with gold . . . And he carved thereon cherubims and palm trees and open flower and covered them with gold fitted upon the carved work." A little hyperbole, you say. Except that the specs with respect to cubits are as detailed as any blueprint today. Not to mention the minutiae on interior decoration.

Today, however, searching for traces of Solomon's temple is forbidden by Muslim officials.

St. Nicholas; Santa Claus; SinterKlass, etc. (b. 270)
From his bones flowed a healing fluid, *manna*, celebrated at The Feast of the Translation of the Relics of St. Nicholas. Maybe this liquid manna was potable; I always understood manna as a foodstuff, more specifically asymmetric crumbly muffins dropping from the sky.

Candy canes commemorate Bishop Nicholas's staff or crozier.

He's patron saint of repentant thieves, brewers, pawnbrokers, and prostitutes. When three maidens were embarking on prostitution, he generously gave them bags of gold coins for the dowries they needed for respectable marriages. As for pawnshops, they sometimes hang golden balls in their windows—representing these three sacks. Oranges in Christmas stockings also reflect these same bags of gold, which is a stretch—and literally, too, since it's not easy to ram an orange into the toe of a long sock.

When a pork butcher killed some children and marinated them, St. Nicholas brought them back to life.

I'm supposed to stick with famous people, and saints don't get much recognition these days—at the moment they get very low Zeitgeist ratings. But you should know of a few that offer practical applications. Here's a half-page list for your Rolodex:

St. Claire (b. 1194) is the patroness of TV (she saw a vision on the wall of her monastic cell).
St. Columbanus (b. 540): patron saint of motorcyclists.
St. Drogo: patron of unattractive people.

St. *Julian*: murderers.

St. Giles: breastfeeding.

St. Vedast: children who are late in learning to walk.

St. Fiacre: hemorrhoids.

St. Denis: headaches.

St.. Polycarp of Smyrna: dysentery.

St. Tryphon: the terrifying scourge of bedbugs.

St. Clotilde, specializing in unmanageable children, and wives with verbally abusive husbands.

Christina the Astonishing: psychiatrists (and the mentally ill) can rely on her assistance.

St. Dymphna (b. 650) also practices in this area, specializing in cases of incest.

Mary Magdalene: hairdressers.

Archangel Gabriel: emergency dispatchers.

St. Balthazar: blackjack dealers. If you're any kind of gambler, he's your man.

St. Bernardino (popular fifteenth-century preacher): patron of advertising and public relations.

St. Isidore: computer coders.

ODDS AND ENDS

This is the end of our oddities.

But not really—because even as we speak there are celebrities out there busy honing their bizarre behavior on the quiet. And the secrets hidden by today's heroes and headliners will come back to haunt them down the road when someone's gleeful Schadenfreude outs them and sets the record straight.

On the other hand, they say there's no such thing as bad publicity. So, here's a fun thought for the 0.00001 of you readers who have achieved renown: you, too, qualify for an entry in a book like this if you have a harebrained habit or unsavory personal history which you keep under wraps as a surprise for a generation to come.

And bear in mind that it's never too late to go weird. Perhaps you're already developing a latent talent for peculiarity. Or perhaps you have yet to identify a promising foible as something you can work with. But whatever your status, good solid effort can net you your own oddness worthy of these pages.

Of course, you follow this absurd advice only if you're a VIP masochist burying an Achilles' heelbone for an archeologist. Besides, this advice doesn't apply to you anyway, because (like me) you're a nobody, and if you're hiding a skeleton in the cupboard, it's not worth the paper this book is written on.

In the end, it's nice to be a nonentity.